LARKIN ABOUT

LARKIN
ABOUT IN COVENTRY

The City where a Great Poet Grew Up

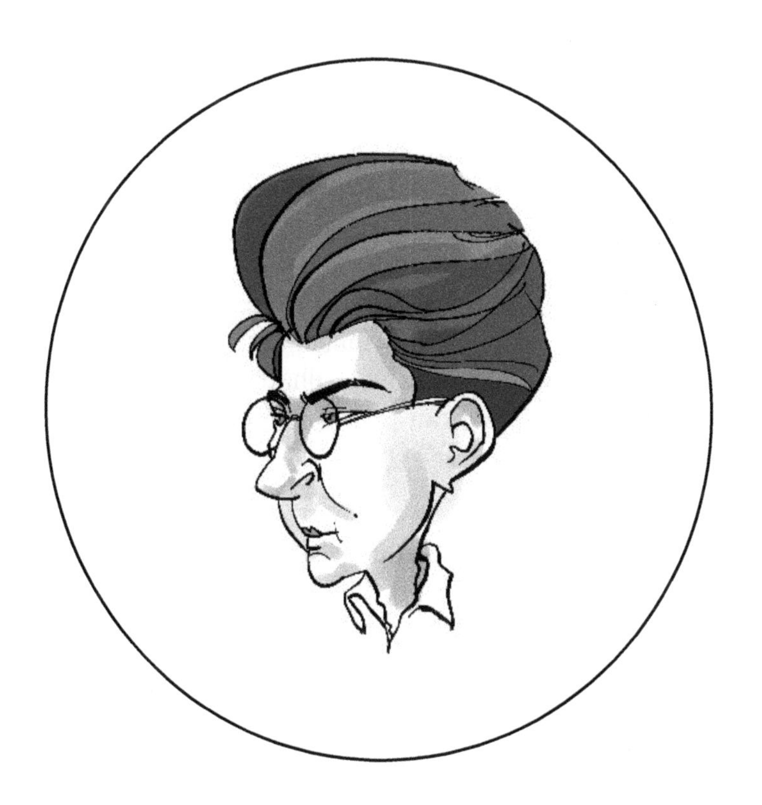

Chris Arnot

This edition published 2018 by:
Takahe Publishing Ltd.
Registered Office:
77 Earlsdon Street, Coventry CV5 6EL

ISBN 978-1-908837-10-3

TAKAHE PUBLISHING LTD.

2018

To many good friends in the next City of Culture

Acknowledgements

Thanks first to Philip Pullen of the Philip Larkin Society who, like Larkin, was born in Coventry and finished up in Hull. His insights have been invaluable – particularly so with regard to the complex relationship between the poet, his family and school friends. I'm also grateful to former WEA lecturer Don Lee, who happens to live in Manchester but seems to know every inch of Coventry that Larkin trod on or looked at while passing by.

Two more Larkin enthusiasts welcomed me to his old school, Henry VIII, and provided me with much information and documentation about his time there. One was Sheila Woolf, former head of English. The other was current librarian and archivist, Helen Cooper, who managed to dig out a great wedge of his school reports. Unlike him, she couldn't have done better.

Adrian Smith, another Henry's old boy who is now emeritus professor of history at Southampton University, provided me with a useful insight into contrasts between Larkin and the Irish poet John Hewitt, influential curator of Coventry's Herbert Art Gallery and Museum in the 1950s and '60s. Gratitude, too, to Martin Roberts, curator of the Herbert today, for giving me a guided tour of Hewitt's legacy, and to Harriet Davidson and Victoria Northridge from the Herbert's History Centre for her help in finding photographs of the Coventry that Larkin would have remembered.

Thanks also to Bill Dunn and David Fry of the Earlsdon Research Group for unearthing so many vintage Earlsdon pictures; to David Wagstaff for his memories and to Chris O'Connell of Theatre Absolute for his input. Not forgetting

Martin Bostock, Kevin and Celia Williams, Satvinder Singh and Cathy Wattebot for letting me into their homes at short notice.

Or indeed Steve Hodder of Takahe Publishing. My publisher may have found new sources of cider since moving away from my local pub, but his copy-reading remains as assiduous as ever.

Last but by no means least, many thanks to two old friends – Peter Dredge for his image of the youthful Philip on the front cover and Peter Walters whose knowledge of this city's fascinating history has proved invaluable. Not to mention the time he has given, despite many other commitments, to tramping the streets and checking the facts.

CONTENTS

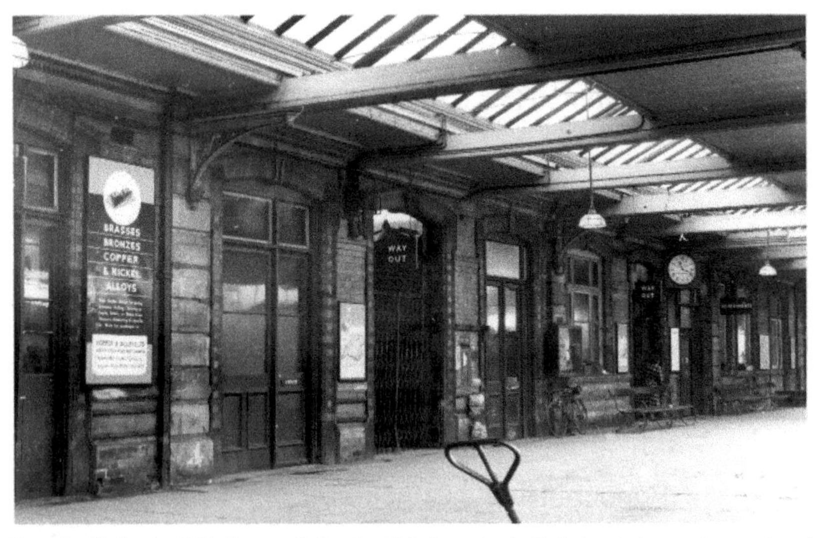

Coventry Station in 1954, the year before Larkin's leaned out of a train window and remembered (Herbert History Centre)

INTRODUCTION

Yes, I remember. I remember being there when the plaque was unveiled on platform one at Coventry Station. It was inscribed with the opening verse of Philip Larkin's poem inspired by a diverted train's brief and unexpected stop at the city where he was born and brought up. I remember that Andrew Davies, the consummate adaptor of literary classics for television, had driven from his home in nearby Kenilworth for the occasion. I remember that Larkin's literary executor Anthony Thwaite had travelled considerably further.

And I remember him saying, "Philip would probably have dismissed it as a lot of hoo-hah. But privately he would have been rather chuffed. Coventry was the place where he spent his first 18 years and he had clear memories of it, good as well as unpleasant."

Music to the ears of my good friend Peter Walters, then of Coventry and Warwickshire Promotions, whose idea it had been to commemorate one of the 20th century's greatest poets in his birthplace. "Hull has had sole rights on Larkin for far too long," he told me at the time.

To be honest, I don't just remember those quotes from Walters and Thwaite word for word. I've read them again, having dug out a yellowing cutting from the cluttered depths of my ancient office filing cabinet. They're included in a piece that I wrote for the Guardian Arts pages that appeared on January 28, 1998.

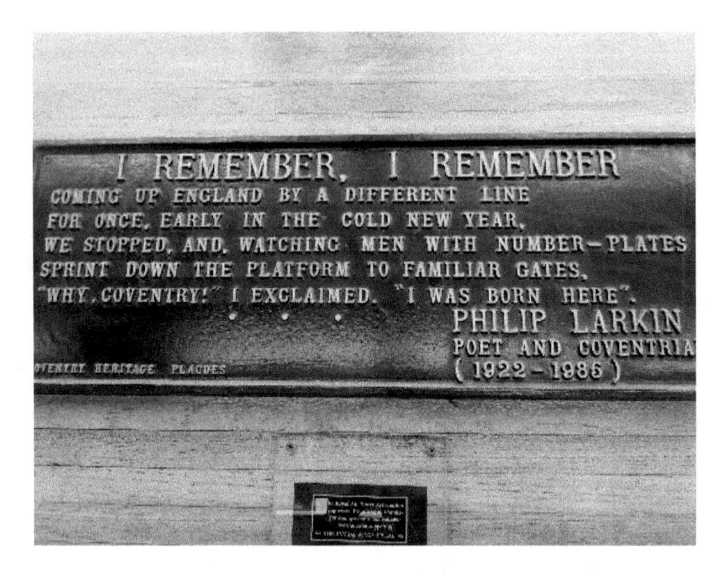

The plaque unveiled on Platform One in 1998

The plaque has since been moved from a low wall close to what has since become yet another branch of Starbucks. It's now screwed to some wooden facing on the other side of the automatic ticket barriers. There it occupies a more elevated position, just to the right of the customer services office with the first-class lounge not far away. Between the two is a metal bowl topped by a message from those rib-ticklers at the Virgin Trains public relations department. "Paws for a refresher," says a sign above the bowl, followed by "Hey there, Rover. Feeling Fur-sty? Have a drink on us."

Heaven knows what Larkin would have made of that. All I do know is that, when he was growing up in Coventry, you could have bought quite a decent car built in one of the many motor factories hereabouts for the price of peak-time first-class ticket to London on a Virgin train today.

Few of those factories have survived. But one is clearly visible as you stroll past the electronic timetables, out of the station forecourt, through lengthy lines of black cabs and then glance to the right. At the far end of Park Road is the rather handsome chunk of red-brick Victoriana that once housed the Quinton Works. Now an Ibis hotel, in Larkin's day it would have been home to the Swift Motor Company and part of his childhood visual landscape, living as he did just round the corner from here in Manor Road.

We shall be visiting his family homes later. All three of them. For now, though, let's walk on towards Greyfriars Green – a far more pleasant stroll than it would have been not so long ago when the route from the station towards the city centre was via a somewhat murky subway. Today it's above ground all the way, through the prospective Friargate Business Quarter, handsomely paved and strewn with benches and saplings, but still very much in its infancy.

A potential building site is bordered by temporary green fences bedecked with images of residents telling us what they love about Coventry. "A city full of potential and talent just waiting to be discovered," is the view of a dancer and performer called Ashley. As if to confirm this view, a young man is currently prancing around nearby, serenaded by rap music from his phone with a tripod camera filming his every step. He's doing a song-and-dance act, or whatever the rap equivalent may be. I make a few attempts to ask him but he's evidently "in the zone" and doesn't want to be interrupted.

Nobody else takes a blind bit of notice. The passers-by are predominantly students. Some appear to be talking to themselves. They are, needless to say, burbling into mobile phones that no longer need to be held up to the ear. Others are relentlessly prodding screens with enviably flexible thumbs. Many are of Asian, African or Caribbean descent.

It doesn't take too much imagination to work out what Larkin would have said about that in a letter to his friend Kingsley Amis. Yes, he was a racist. But then most white British folk old enough to remember when we still had a sizeable empire tended to look down on black and Asian people. I had more than enough arguments on the subject with people of his generation, including my own parents, when I was a student in the late 1960s. And for some time after that.

We shouldn't forget what Larkin wrote about his "Mum and Dad" in the opening lines of This Be the Verse. And I suspect that you're more fucked up than most if your Dad harboured an admiration for Adolf Hitler and took you on holidays to Germany in the 1930s. Sydney Larkin was the City Treasurer and kept a model of the Fuhrer on the mantelpiece of his office in the Council House until told to remove it, along with other Nazi regalia, shortly before the outbreak of war. It may be that Sydney changed his views somewhat after doing his share of fire extinguishing in the wake of the blitz that destroyed much of the mediaeval centre of Coventry on November 14, 1940. Not to mention the follow-up bombing over four nights in April 1941 that damaged the family home as well as Philip's school.

Ask me what I love about Coventry today and I'd say that it's a city of cultures, full of people from somewhere else with good stories to tell. The accents in my local "social" (formerly "working men's") club range from Irish and Scottish to Geordie, Welsh and West Indian. Even Cockney in one case. They're predominantly older Coventrians who came here to work in the factories, to lay down the ring road or simply to help to rebuild the city in the post-war years.

The latest generation of incomers have largely come because of two thriving universities. Despite its misleading name, Warwick University is within the boundaries of Coventry. It frequently features in the tables as the highest performing English university outside Oxbridge, London and Durham. Very popular with the Chinese, among others. Coventry University, meanwhile, is the highest performing former polytechnic. What's more, it's bang in the centre of a city that its popularity is helping to transform. Student apartment blocks are mushrooming in most unlikely places, including the site of the former Larkin residence near the station. They're giving Coventry a youthful vibrancy that has finally put the 'Ghost Town' label to bed, as well as a diversity that helped to secure its role as the next City of Culture. After Hull, as it happens.

To ponder what Larkin would have made of that I didn't just shrug and gaze heavenwards. I took a day return to Hull and back and, after pausing to admire the statue of Larkin on the station concourse, had a lengthy lunchtime chat in the bar of the Royal Station Hotel with Philip Pullen. Like the other Philip, he was born and brought up in Coventry but finished up living on Humberside where he is now a prominent member of the Philip Larkin Society as well as author of several insightful papers on the poet's relationship with his birthplace and indeed his family. On the specific issue of the City of Culture title being bestowed on the two places where Larkin spent most of his life he had this to say:

"His public persona would have thrown his hands in the air and made some disparaging comments . . . Secretly, however, I think he would have been rather pleased."

Which seemed to echo Anthony Thwaite's comments about Larkin's likely reaction to the plaque on Coventry Station. It confirmed my growing suspicion that there was more than one Philip Larkin. Behind the lugubrious and curmudgeonly facade was a much more sensitive, polite and humorous soul who wanted to be remembered for his ability spin words into memorable verses of rare beauty and perception.

But this book is not going to be yet another analytical autobiography about his character and motivation. It's really about the place that will become the UK's City of Culture in 2021, almost a century after his birth here. By then it will be 40 years since I moved to Coventry with my wife and three small children. Having been a national freelance for the past three of those four decades, the station behind us has been my gateway to the world. Yes, I've lived in other places, including Birmingham and Nottingham, Ludlow and London. And, yes, I still catch regular Virgin Trains to the capital. Not first class, mind you, and not peak-time if I can help it. The 10.31 usually has me pulling into Euston in exactly an hour for a cost of just over 30 quid – admittedly with a senior rail card.

This short walk across Friargate is part of my standard ritual some 30 minutes before boarding. Shunning the lure of

Starbucks on platform one, I head for Finney's on the far side of Greyfriar's Green. It's a stylish coffee bar that does a strong Americano with a decent crema. The Green itself has flowerbeds ablaze with blooms of many colours for much of the year.

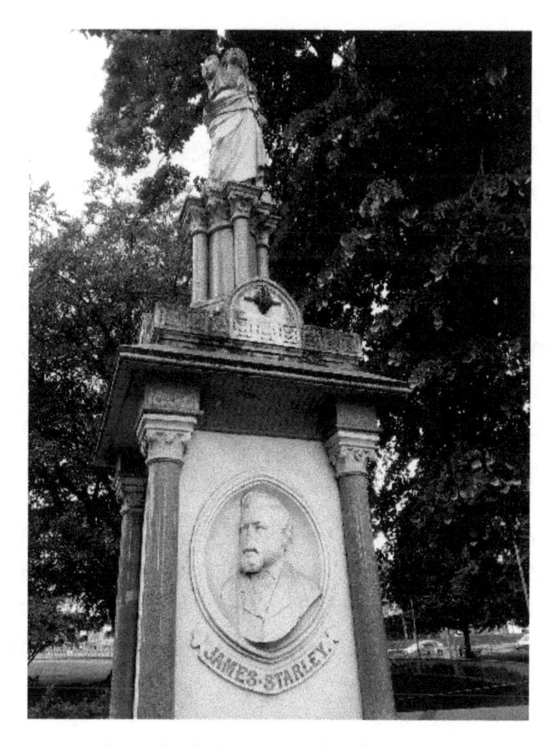

James Starley's statue on Greyfriars Green

To the right is Starley's statue commemorating James Starley, father of the bicycle industry, who sent himself to Coventry in the early 1860s. For some reason, the monument to his memory is topped by an armless Roman senator -- like Venus only less shapely. The arms appear to have been amputated at one time or another, along with Starley's nose.

Still, the well-used cycle track that passes close by seems an appropriate tribute to his legacy, even if it does dip within a hundred yards or so down an underpass beneath four lanes of motor traffic on the ring road that flattened the Larkin family home.

It's far more restful on the eyes to gaze out from Finney's over the green towards The Quadrant, built around 1860 in neo-classical style, and the city's finest surviving example of terraced housing for the prosperous middle classes. There's a plaque on Number One pointing out that Angela Brazil "lived and worked here from 1911 to 1947". She too was a writer, albeit of jolly hockey-stick stories about girls' boarding schools. Whether the Larkins knew the Brazils is debatable, but Philip almost certainly knew Angela's work. While still at Oxford he parodied her style, or something very much like it, in Trouble at Willow Gables.

Today The Quadrant largely houses solicitors and accountants. Across the Green, meanwhile, there are rows of estate agents. One of them, Loveitts, is housed in the former school of one Mary Ann Evans, better known as George Eliot.

Not far from Finney's front window is what looks like an ancient horse trough full of plants and inscribed with a plaque to the memory of the novelist's mentor, Charles Bray, and his wife Caroline. He was a prosperous ribbon manufacturer who owned the Coventry Herald newspaper. She was another children's writer and an active campaigner against animal cruelty. The Brays' home, "Rosehill", was the gathering place for the Rosehill Circle, a haven for free thinkers with radical opinions. Among them were the social reformer Robert Owen, the philosopher Herbert Spencer and the social theorist and writer Harriet Martineau. Oh yes, and George Eliot.

Her most celebrated novel is set against the disquiet caused by the coming of the railway in the 1830s. Now this city's first station was opened in 1838. So was Middlemarch really Coventry? Or were there elements of Coventry in Middlemarch? The novel, that is, not the evocative 1994 television adaptation by the aforesaid Andrew Davies which had to be filmed elsewhere for obvious reasons.

We could spend pages discussing that. But let's stay focused on one of the great poets of the 20th century rather than one of the most acclaimed novelists of the 19th. The city that Larkin returned to shortly after it was shattered by the Luftwaffe had been written off before. And since.

It happened for economic rather than military reasons when I arrived here in 1981 to take a job as features editor and columnist on what was then the Evening Telegraph. Local band The Specials had shot to number one with Ghost Town, a song written in Glasgow that caught the mood of the times throughout the UK. National journalists, however, found it a convenient label for Coventry. They were taking day returns from London to write the city's obituary as one factory after another closed down. But Coventry has a habit of reinventing itself and right now it's going through that process again. Something to examine closer, perhaps, as the city of Larkin's birth approaches its time in the sun as the UK's City of Culture.

To misquote the last line of I Remember, I Remember, something, like nothing, happens anywhere.

CHAPTER ONE

Born in a Council House

It was just after 10.30 on a Monday morning and a familiar broad-browed and bespectacled face was peering down quizzically from a sign on the side of a mock-Tudor pub on Corporation Street as if to sigh, "What am I doing up here"?

Short answer: because the hostelry formerly known as the Tudor Rose and before that the Tally Ho had recently been re-named The Philip Larkin. Those of us who have been asking for more "Larkinalia" in Coventry shouldn't complain. Though I suspect that the poet might have felt more at home attached to the Golden Cross, a hostelry with some genuine Tudor parts on the corner of cobbled Hay Lane in the nearby Cathedral Quarter. He used to go there in his late teens, sometimes with friends and sometimes alone, to browse through books borrowed from what was then the nearby central library while surreptitiously ogling the barmaid.

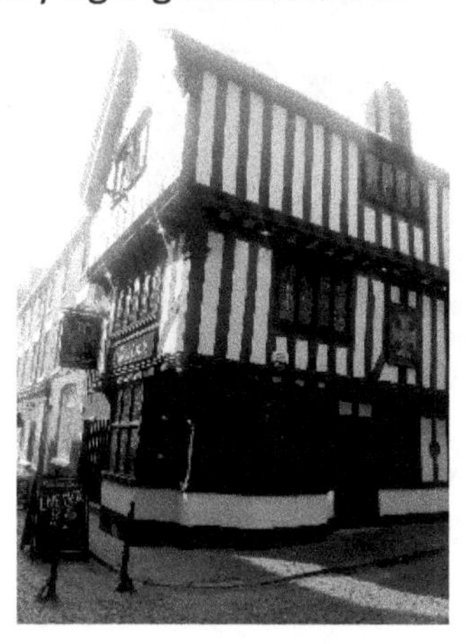

Larkin's favourite Coventry pub, a few yards from the central library

And, yes, he did like a drink. Admitted as much in one or more of God knows how many letters being edited for publication by Hull-based academics and enthusiasts. I remember being shown one by Professor James Booth, then head of English at the university and more recently author of Philip Larkin, Life Art and Love (Bloomsbury). Like many another, the letter was from Philip to his mother, Eva, and written in May, 1976, the year before she died. It began "Dearest Old Creature" before going on to say, "I am slowly recovering from my visit to London and my recording of Desert Island Discs. I didn't think it went at all well, principally because I was very nervous. If only I could have had a few double gins beforehand."

Well, I like a drink too. But not at 10.30 in the morning, thanks very much. No such qualms from other "early-doors" customers at the Philip Larkin here on the corner of Corporation Street and the Burges. Some were already into the first of the day. Or was it the second or third? After all, the pub had been

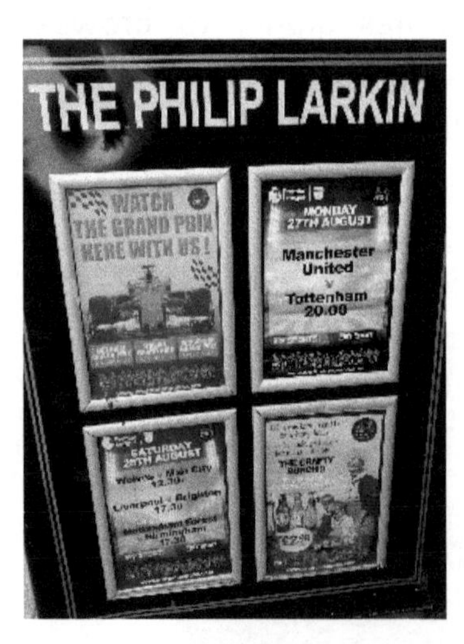

The Philip Larkin pub, offering the Premier League and the Grand Prix

open since 9 am, the start of the working day for many a shop assistant or office worker. Admittedly, the clientele in here tended to be of mature years, apart from a trio of youngsters checking their phones under a big screen – one of many already showing the odds for the 3.25 at Plumpton. Had I been here yesterday afternoon, the screens would have been transmitting live coverage of Manchester United v Chelsea with extensive analysis before and after.

Strolling up to the bar, I asked for an Americano. The barman couldn't have looked more surprised if I'd called for a glass of Prosecco with a cherry. "A what?"

"An Americano."

This time something seemed to register. He approached the coffee machine warily and scanned the options before triumphantly turning to inform me that there was no milk.

"I don't want milk, thanks. I like it black."

There was a grunted response before a mug of coffee was finally forthcoming. I thought better of asking for a glass of soda water with ice and lemon to go with it. Instead I asked to speak to the licensee. The barman gestured towards a man with a shaved head and a tattooed neck at the far end of the bar.

Leroy Blake proved surprisingly receptive when I asked what he knew about Larkin. "I know what his Mum and Dad did to him," he grinned. "Made me laugh that did . . . Oh yeah, and I read the one that features on that plaque on the station. Enjoyed it, too."

"I knew he was a poet born in Coventry," put in a man on my side of the bar with many earrings but no front teeth.

"Ever read any of his poems?"

He shook his head and I shook his hand. At least he knew who Larkin was. I suspect that had I asked some of the regulars about George Eliot someone would come up with, "Didn't he play left-side midfield for the City?"

Instead I took my coffee to a seat in the corner, glancing through the window at an imposing building diagonally across the street. The Old Grammar School is a Grade-1 listed sandstone structure built in the 1340s as the Hospital of St John. It was transformed into a school in 1550 and named after Henry VIII, who had expired three years earlier. Damaged in the blitz of April, 1941, this architectural gem lay dormant for decades until it was finally restored in 2014-15 as part of the nearby Transport Museum. It now hosts conferences, dinners, networking events and even weddings.

And the Larkin connection?

Well, he went to what you might call the "new grammar school". In 1885 teachers and pupils moved out of town to a more expansive site on Warwick Road, and that was where young Philip began his secondary education some 45 or so years later. We shall be returning to his school days in another chapter. For now we're off to see The Birthplace, as it would be called were this Shakespeare's Stratford rather than Larkin's Coventry. We have a bus to catch.

The stop is just outside a bookie's some 50 yards or so from the entrance to the pub named after him. There's another sign with the same head-and-shoulders portrait on this side. Am I imagining it or is he peering down on the Burges with something approaching distaste?

It would have been considerably more upmarket in his childhood. When he was nine or ten in the early 1930s, one side of this narrow, mediaeval thoroughfare was knocked down to make it wider and allow traffic to swing round to the left into the new Corporation Street. Long before the Luftwaffe bombarded the ancient city centre, the local authority was already bent on making it more amenable to the motor car. After all, Coventry had played a key part in its development, as well as that of the bicycle, as the Transport Museum displays in such an engaging way.

There seem to be a disproportionate number of bookies on this, the 1930s side of the Burges. But standing by the bus stop I can see that the distinctive mediaeval roofscape across the street is still very much intact. What's more, plans have been approved to improve the shop frontages. Initial funding has already been secured from Historic England. More money may be coming from the Heritage Lottery Fund.

The scheme includes a proposal to open up the area beyond an arched alleyway where very uneven cobbles currently lead to a glimpse of a somewhat stagnant River Sherbourne, hemmed in by railings, barbed wire and banks covered with an abundance of brambles, nettles and weeds.

The potential is all too evident. Mediaeval roofscapes appear even more . . . well, mediaeval when viewed from the rear. Two of Coventry's famous three spires seem to peer over far more recent roofscapes. The plan is to even up the cobbles, open up the river, provide steps for passers-by to sit upon and gaze upon the water and – hopefully – to persuade restaurants and bars to provide outside tables and chairs for the summer months.

Plans like this have been mooted before. This time, however, they are more than likely to materialise. The man behind the scheme is Ian Harrabin of Complex Development Projects, based in London but very involved in Coventry.

He was born here. A "Coventry kid", as they say in these parts. Harrabin is chair of the Historic Coventry Trust that has secured £4.3 million of lottery funding to open up to the public the substantial remains of the Charterhouse, a former monastery founded in 1385 by Richard II. Adorned by spectacular wall paintings, it's set in 70 acres of parkland within the city boundaries.

And it was Harrabin's company (let's call it CDP) that handsomely restored so many mediaeval survivors in Far Gosford Street in the city's former silk and ribbon-waving area. Somehow they had survived not only the blitz but also the modernist and neo-brutalist eras. It was also CDP that linked the old Cathedral Quarter to the new Millennium Square (circa 2000) with Priory Place, an imaginative mixture of ancient and modern buildings that includes the excavated ruins of St Mary's, the first of three cathedrals to serve Coventry, as well as the remains of the Saxon church that preceded it. Not to mention a visitors' centre with an undercroft housing many more historical artefacts, a once-derelict 1850s ribbon factory converted into loft apartments, a branch of Nando's surrounded by exotic pots, an impressive array of Oriental restaurants – Chinese, Japanese, Korean and Vietnamese – as well as the studios of BBC Coventry and Warwickshire.

Larkin is remembered a few yards from the studio entrance in The Walk of Fame, a line of engraved paving dedicated to Coventrians who have made their mark nationally and, in some cases, internationally. He's between the actor Billie Whitelaw and the runner Dave Moorcroft.

(Let's imagine that the poet were to come back today and be interviewed on CWR after "a few large gins". Would he make some disparaging remarks about the restaurants opposite? Probably not. The late Jean Hartley, who co-published his first books of poetry with her husband George, one told me that he often went for a three-course "businessman's lunch" at Hull's first Chinese restaurant that opened amid much excitement in the early 1960s. Any comment about the number of "Chinks" in Coventry would be kept for one of his letters to Kingsley Amis. Casual racism was par for the course in their day, even for literary figures who'd enjoyed the benefit of an Oxford education.)

Now, in case you were wondering, the bus to The Birthplace had finally arrived. We'd swept round from the Burges into Corporation Street and there on the next corner, where the bus swept round again to the right, stood the place where I worked for most of the 1980s.

The Coventry Evening Telegraph was based in a classic

1950s building that doubled, in parts, as a pied-à-terre for the newspaper's owner, Lord Iliffe. His apartment is still in there somewhere. And will stay, albeit somewhat updated, when this one-time haven of hacks [surely "fearless organ of truth", ed] is redesigned as a "boutique" hotel. With a cocktail bar, if you please.

There's more. "The old newsroom is going to be a banqueting hall," I was told by Ian Harrabin. Yes, him again. This project is another Complex Development.

Our old lair, once fuggy with cigarette smoke and resounding with shouts and "copy" (and sometimes "coffee") over the clatter of heavy typewriters, will soon be serving food considerably more refined than bacon batches ferried from the canteen by messenger "boys" and "girls". And the former print room, once heady with the smell of ink and the thunder of hot-metal, is going to be transformed into an art-house cinema.

"We're going to have a rooftop bar as well," Ian confided before adding dryly: "That should be open at least five days a year." (Or more if the summer of 2018 was anything to go by.) Al fresco drinkers will be able to look across the road at the Belgrade, the first civic theatre to be built in the UK after the Second World War and something of a pioneer in its day. Theatre-in-education began there. Trevor Nunn cut his teeth there before moving to the RSC in Stratford. The [Arnold] Wesker Trilogy made its debut there before transferring to London.

These days the more cutting-edge works tend to be confined to the B2 studio. There are nearby alternatives, however. The Warwick University Arts Centre for one. Okay, it's on the edge of town and you have to park in an adjoining multi-storey, which can make it feel a bit like a cultural hypermarket. Still, it offers not only cutting-edge theatre but also cinema, art-house as well as mainstream. And smack in the middle of town is Theatre Absolute, the UK's first shop-front theatre, opened by local playwright Chris O'Connell and his partner Julia Negus in a former chip shop once known as Fishy Moore's. No fancy scenery and elaborate lighting there; just thought-provoking work by Chris and others.

But that's based further down Corporation Street, on the corner of City Arcade, while our bus, having turned sharp right at the Belgrade, was heading past a cluster of chain restaurants and under the ring road. Yet another Complex Development Project will see the former gas works site on the other side partially covered by what Harrabin had described as private-sector apartments "of high quality". In a much greener landscape, what's more. His company's plans include opening up and extending the brook in nearby Naul's Mill Park so that it flows under the ring road to link up with the Belgrade Plaza.

Fair play to him, as they say round here. Few have done more to ensure that Coventry will be spruced up and ready to take a bow as City of Culture by 2021. By that time, incidentally, it will be 99 years since Larkin was born a mile or so up the road from what is now the urban wasteland that once housed the gasworks.

Soon the bus began to pass through mundane suburbia close to the Canal Basin where the Coventry Telegraph (no longer "Evening") has re-located to smaller premises. Here on the main road there was a derelict pub, a Greek restaurant, rows of shops and takeaways, bingo hall, former working men's club. And so on. There's a school, Barr's Hill, where Larkin's sister Kitty was a pupil back in the days when it was a girls' grammar. The writer Susan Hill also went there, albeit in the post-war years.

We were en route to Radford, once home of Daimler and several more motor companies as well as the Larkin family. Sydney and Eva moved there with Kitty in 1919. Philip was born at the house three years later – on August 9, 1922, to be precise, weighing in at 10 lbs with a fine head of dark hair.

Number 2 Poultney Road was a council house insofar as the City Council owned it. As we know, Sydney was City Treasurer and would soon be aspiring to somewhere bigger and better. He would have been horrified to have been living here when the garden village that Radford began as rapidly expanded into a vast council estate during the 1930s.

Mind you, Poultney Road stands on the edge of that now largely privately owned estate, separated from the main Radford Road by a green harbouring a children's play area. There's also a pleasant little copse of mature trees encircled by a hedge.

Number two was rather tucked away beyond a double gate leading to an expansive parking area and a crunchy stone path. There was a little wooden rocking chair for two outside a window with the blinds pulled down.

No bell and no knocker on a front door with a rather twee lamp on the side. So I hammered on the uPVC which brought an immediate response. A furiously barking dog hurled itself at the door. Nobody came to open it, however. So I stepped back and noticed that the stone cladding had gone. The brickwork was covered in it last time I was here, shortly before the Larkin celebration on the station 20 years ago. On that occasion the previous owner was at home. Pleasant and friendly chap as it turned out. I remember asking him how he'd feel about having a blue plaque on the side of his residence in memory of the great poet who had been born there.

"I wouldn't mind," he mused, "as long as it didn't spoil the cladding."

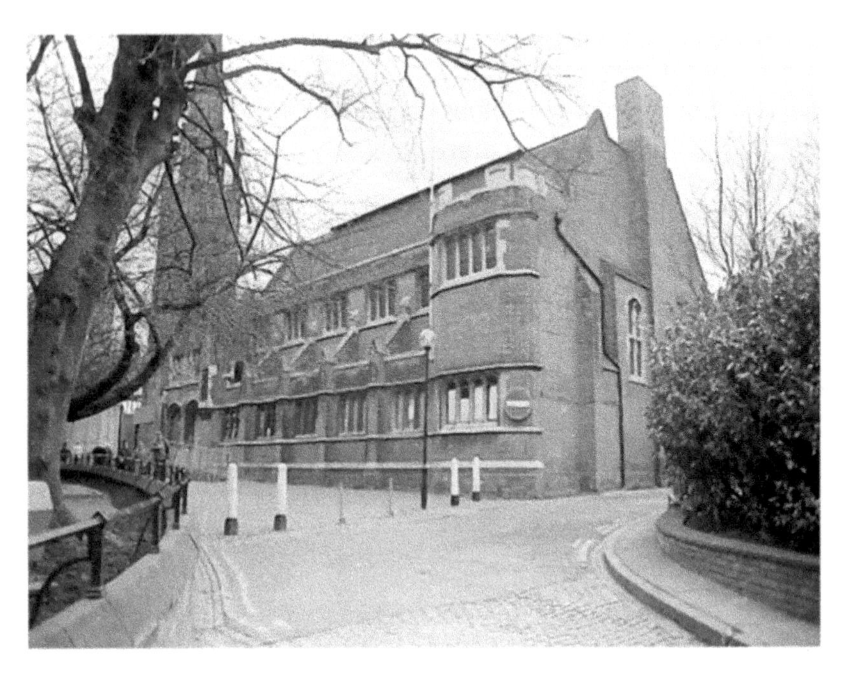

What was left of Larkin's beloved central library shortly before it closed in 1986 and moved to a building that once housed the Locarno dance hall (Earlsdon Research Group)

CHAPTER 2

Christened in a Cathedral

No stone cladding on the second Larkin house in Barras Lane. No blue plaque either. But then the family only lived there for a couple of years in the mid-1920s. "Just as well," said the current owner, Martin Bostock, gesturing towards the nearby junction with the main Holyhead Road. "Within a few years, that would become one of the worst bottlenecks in Britain. The traffic heading from London to Birmingham or on to Manchester or Glasgow came this way."

That was long before the advent of motorways, of course. Not to mention the four-lane ring road that did what the Luftwaffe had somehow failed to do by flattening the third and final Larkin home in Coventry. We shall be visiting the site of Penvorn on Manor Road and discovering more about Philip's childhood and adolescence there in the next chapter.

Here on Barras Lane, meanwhile, there's something rather fortress-like about the former short-term Chateau Larkin, standing as it does at the top end of a sloping path behind a high sandstone wall. Somehow I suspect that wall would have appealed to Sydney. It gave the impression of keeping the "hoi-polloi" at bay.

"For some time after he moved the family on, this area remained one of the last gasps of the middle-classes in the inner-city," said Martin who works from home on economic development projects and seems to be quite knowledgeable about the neighbourhood. "Residents here were inventors, engineers, head draftsmen and managers. A guy who lived just a few doors away until comparatively recently was the retired chief engineer at Dunlop who had invented the predecessor to aircraft undercarriages many years previously."

Martin bought number 61 from a now retired expert in fine art from Warwick University and gave the impression that he had no intention of moving on himself any time soon. "I don't know whether Sydney Larkin knew this but the house was unusual for its time – quite austere architecturally for an Edwardian place built in 1908. There are no mouldings and even the hallway tiles are comparatively restrained. The rooms are all rectangles with comparatively low ceilings. And very little has changed since his family lived here. All the woodwork, including the front fireplace surround, is still the same. Same open fires; same doors; same walls," he added, leading the way through to a kitchen where only the microwave and fridge were comparative newcomers. There was even a bell to summon servants in the "middle room" between lounge and kitchen.

Beyond the kitchen window sprawled the back yard of a comparatively modern intruder: the Days Inn Hotel. "The security cameras are quite reassuring as this area has changed a lot," Martin went on. "Most of the big houses are now sub-divided. There are a couple of bail hostels nearby and there was – not sure if it's still there – a place for former sex workers coming off crack cocaine."

All the same, I had the sense that he not only enjoyed living in the five-bedroom house that he shared with two of his sons but also liked the idea that a famous poet had lived here, however fleetingly. "Yes, I like his poetry. Although it's not cheerful, it does make you think. He was obviously very introspective, which is why so much is still being mined out about him . . . He was evidently a complex person."

Too right, I was thinking to myself as I bade farewell and set off for a nose about the neighbourhood, an all too typical Coventry mixture of the mundane and the intriguing. (Yes, that mixture is to be found in most cities but it seems particularly prevalent here, perhaps because of the combination of a rich history with a turbulent 20th century.)

Just beyond a hair and nail salon and Son of a Gunn [sic] Tattoos was a blue plaque. Not to Philip Larkin, needless to say, but to Bahne Bonniksen, inventor of the Karrusel movement for watches (1894). And round the corner in Upper Spon Street the quaintly half-timbered Weaver's House (dating back to the 1540s and open to the public on certain days) looked out over an estate of 1960s concrete social housing. Weaving is . . . well, woven into Coventry's heritage. As indeed is watch-making, particularly in the nearby districts of Chapelfields and Earlsdon. Indeed the office where I'm writing this is in a loft in the heart of Earlsdon that would once have housed somebody bent over the workings of an intricate ticker while squinting through an eye glass

Back on the corner of Barras Lane and Holyhead Road was the spot where William Turner positioned himself to sketch the three spires of Coventry in 1830. Or so Martin reckoned.

As it happens, that picture is framed on a landing wall just below this office-loft. Not the original, alas. But it said something about Coventry's importance at the time that a lifelong Londoner who painted so many evocative pictures at sea took the trouble to travel to the centre of England to capture such a scene.

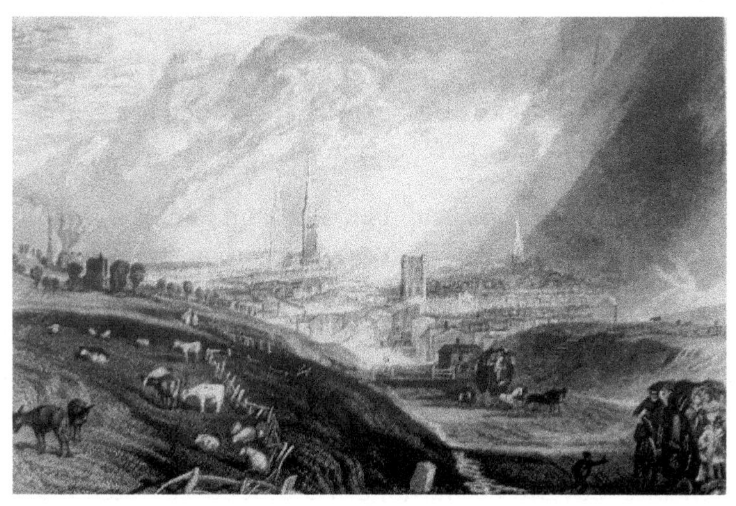

JMW Turner's view of Coventry from a spot close to the site of the second Larkin family house

Alfred Lord Tennyson was also "in-spired", as it were, by a fleeting visit to the city in 1840. His characteristically lengthy tribute to Godiva has a short introduction in which he explains how, while waiting for a London-bound train, he "hung with grooms and porters on the bridge to watch the three tall spires".

That was the bridge, incidentally, that Larkin walked across on his way to Henry VIII School, some 100 yards or so up the road. Four times a day he would have trudged to and fro past

Tennyson's vantage point. Why? Because he used to go home for lunch.

Finding a sighting of all three spires from that bridge today proved impossible. Too many tall and block-like post-war buildings in between. The nearest uninterrupted view is from across the road, between Burger King and American Golf on the edge of the Central Six Retail Park.

Only one of those spires still has a church attached to it. Holy Trinity stands at the point where the central square of Broadgate gives way to the Cathedral Quarter. To the right, as you approach the church, is a branch of Wilko's at the back of the Cathedral Lanes Shopping Centre. To the left are the black and white Lychgate Cottages, near the gate through which coffins were carried into the churchyard. Built as recently as 1648, some of the timbers used on the cottages have been tree-ring dated to 1414. Beautifully bent and weathered timbers they are when viewed close up. From a distance they appear to blend seamlessly with the adjoining mock-Tudor pub, built in the 1930s and now yet another outlet for J D Wetherspoon's. What was I saying about the intriguing and the mundane?

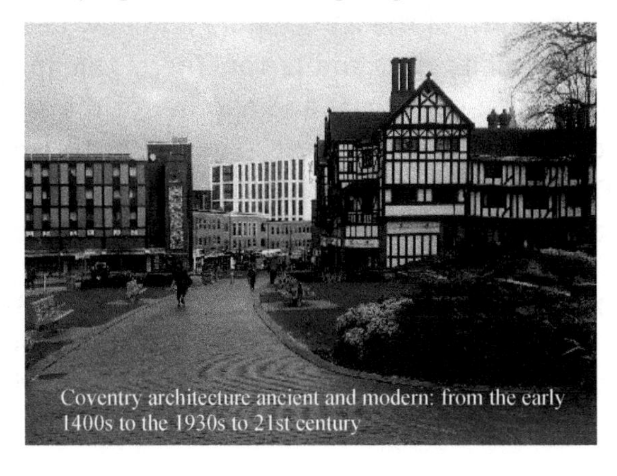

Coventry architecture ancient and modern: from the early 1400s to the 1930s to 21st century

Larkin may not have had much in the way of religious conviction but he evidently liked visiting religious buildings, as he revealed in his poem Church Going. First published in 1955, it was already asking the question: what are we going to do with these buildings when they fall out of use completely?

He would certainly have known Holy Trinity. May even have known that the Shakespearean actress Sarah Siddons was married there in 1773, that George Eliot's father Robert Evans was a plate-bearer in the 1840s and that the church harboured one of the last three untouched charnel houses in England. Still does. Having left Coventry for Oxford by then, Larkin probably never knew about the valiant role played by the vicar and his family in putting out incendiaries at the height of the 1940 blitz. The original windows were blown out, however. Stunning stained-glass replacements were forthcoming in the post-war years, paid for by contributions from couples who were married there. Quite a sight, particularly when lit up by the sun.

Sunlight also helps to illuminate the mediaeval Doom Painting, one of the best preserved Last Judgement Day art-works in Britain. Dating from around 1435, it was painstakingly restored at the turn of the 21st century and now bestrides the chancel arch in all its glory and terror. There's an image of the Virgin Mary baring her breast and another of the entrance to Hell depicted as a gaping mouth. The art historian Andrew Graham-Dixon has described the painting as "one of the most important discoveries ever made in the field of mediaeval art".

Holy Trinity is a building of cathedral-like proportions. On a hill too, unlike the even bigger St Mary's, built on the site of a church founded by Leofric and Godiva and once sprawling down the slope that is now Priory Place. The building was destroyed during the Dissolution of the Monasteries in the early 1540s and not replaced as the city's official cathedral for nigh-on four centuries. Cathedral status was finally bestowed on nearby St Michael's in 1918. It would survive from the end of one world war until the early stages of the next. Philip Larkin was christened there in the meantime.

Just over 10 years later, J B Priestley arrived en route between the Cotswolds and the Black Country on his English Journey. He must have been on the cobbled streets between the spires of Holy Trinity and St Michael's, when he marvelled how at "genuinely old and picturesque" this part of the city centre appeared before going on to observe, "You peep round a corner and see half-timbered and gabled houses that would do for the second act of the Meistersinger. In fact, you could stage the Meistersinger – or film it – in Coventry."

Believe it or not, that's still true today. Indeed Wagner's opera could be staged in the cathedral ruins for anybody with four and a half hours to spare. Many dramatic events have been, from touring Shakespeare productions to the Coventry mediaeval mystery plays as well as contemporary works by playwrights with local connections. In 1997 and 2018 actors from the Teatr Biuro Podrozy in Poland strode around on stilts in that windowless and roofless space. Their faces were hidden behind leather masks as they set out to evoke fear and helplessness in a war zone.

Quite appropriate, needless to say. After all, this area had been at the heart of a war zone 57 years previously. And yet . .

. and yet . . . you can still stand just beyond the Golden Cross pub that Larkin frequented in his adolescence, peer down the cobbles of Bayley Lane and take in a view not too dissimilar to that savoured by Priestley on his pre-war sojourn.

Okay, there are a couple of comparatively modern intruders – a restaurant at the top and the extension to the Herbert Art Gallery at the far end. But the cobbles wind their way around two splendid half-timbered examples of late 18th and early 19th century re-fronting of much older buildings. Beyond them is the entrance to St Mary's Hall, one of the finest surviving mediaeval guild halls in the country, harbouring a magnificent nine-metres by three tapestry depicting 75 individual characters, including members of the royal court, angels, saints and apostles. At its centre is the Virgin Mary and around the edge are assorted dogs, dragons, demons and mice. Extraordinarily, it still hangs in the same wall that it was created for at the end of the 1400s when Coventry was a city wealthy enough to pay for the skills of Flemish weavers.

It was here at St Mary's Hall that Henry VI and Margaret of Anjou briefly held court in the 1450s; here that Elizabeth 1 had Mary Queen of Scots briefly imprisoned in 1569; here that George Eliot set the trial scene in her first novel, Adam Bede. And it was here that Philip Larkin returned to from Hull in 1978 to receive the Coventry Award of Merit along with Bishop Cuthbert Bardsley and Jack Jones of the Transport and General Workers' Union.

Further along the cobbles stands the elegantly pillared Drapers' Hall, built in the 1830s in Greek Revival style and about to be revived, restored and reopened for the first time in nigh-on 30 years as a music venue. Not just any old music either. Classical music, if you don't mind. The highly regarded Renaissance and Baroque choir and orchestra, Armonico Consort, are mooted to be moving there from their current residence 10 miles down the road in Warwick.

There will also be educational facilities for music students at the nearby university as well as schoolchildren elsewhere in the city. A £1 million grant has been forthcoming from Arts Council England and Prince Charles has chipped in some more through his regeneration trust.

As the name suggests, Drapers' Hall was a gathering place for drapers. The most important of Coventry's mediaeval guilds, they were still going strong not only in the 1830s but in the 1930s when, as City Treasurer, Sydney Larkin would almost certainly have been invited to dinner-dances in that sumptuous hall with his wife Eva. His office was just around the corner in the Council House, built during the First World War in the style of a grandiose 16th century mansion and somehow surviving the Second with nothing much more than blown-out windows and shrapnel marks on its sumptuous frontage.

The cathedral of St Michael's did not survive, needless to say. Apart from the Gothic spire, that is. It still soars over Bayley Lane to a height of 295 ft. Only Salisbury and Norwich are higher among English cathedrals. Quite a climb to the summit, I can report, having once done it with two of my grandchildren. Worth it, mind you, for the view from the top.

Back at ground level, those majestic outer walls, those window frames harbouring only fragments of glass, those wide open spaces never cease to move me, no matter how often I visit. Neither do the words "Father Forgive", later transcribed on the surviving stonework of the sanctuary. Nor the Charred Cross created from two of the great fallen oak beams, bound together by the cathedral's stonemason Jock Forbes after he'd spent the night of November 14, 1940, fighting fires.

And, like Larkin, I am not a religious man.

Beneath one of the huge, gaunt window frames of the ruins lies a rare survivor of that terrible night – the statue and tomb of the splendidly named Bishop Huyshe Wolcott Yeatman-Biggs. He died in 1922, the year young Philip was christened here. One of the bishop's hands is clasping a small model of the cathedral. Did the poet have that image at the back of his mind when he wrote An Arundel Tomb with its inspiring last line, all too typically qualified by the line before?

Probably not. He was in Chichester not Coventry when the muse came. Still, childhood images tend to linger long in the memory when death is the subject in mind.

Yes, of course, that was pure speculation. You might as well ask whether Shakespeare was a regular visitor to St Mary's Hall and, indeed, whether he performed there in his youth. A carved likeness of his face peers pensively at the entrance to the hall from a surviving wall of the old cathedral opposite. Yet much of the Bard's life is shrouded in mystery. All we know for certain is that Coventry was the nearest major city to the town where he spent his childhood, youth and old age. Oh yes, and he set the opening scene of Richard II on Gosford Green, a mile or so up the road from the Cathedral Quarter.

We also know (well, some of us do) that the Charred Cross has been moved from the ruins of St Michael's to the adjoining "new" Cathedral where it can be more safely displayed. And, yes, we shall be returning to Sir Basil Spence's architectural masterpiece in a later chapter.

In the meantime we still have to go in search of the third and final spire. Before setting off, however, there should be time for a quick one in Drapers. No, not Drapers' Hall but Drapers' cafe-bar, built at the dawn of the 21st century in 1950s style to mirror some of the post-war modernist structures around it. On a fine summer's day or early evening, however, the bar's first-floor rear terrace is a good place to sit with a beer or a coffee overlooking the ruins and the survivors from much earlier times. A reminder, if ever there was one, that this is a city not just of invention but of re-invention.

Never write it off.

CHAPTER 3

Lived in Fear

It was, of course, a coincidence that Sydney Larkin's place of work survived the blitz of November 14, 1940, as well as the house where he had moved in with his family 13 years previously. I don't suppose that Hermann Goering had a word with the Luftwaffe before they set off on that moonlit night and told them, "Do not, under any circumstances, destroy Penvorn on the end of Manor Road or the Council House on Earl Street. A fervent supporter of National Socialism lives in one and works in the other. He is the City Treasurer, no less, and could be very useful to us as our man in the Midlands when the United Kingdom finally becomes part of a united Germany . . . "

Sydney's office, bedecked with Nazi regalia and harbouring that model of Hitler until shortly before the outbreak of war, was housed in the upper reaches of Coventry's ornately imposing civic centre. He was on a level with the statues of Leofric and Godiva.

Outside his window was a balcony. The teenage Philip would join him there during the city's annual Godiva Procession. Father and son would leer down on whichever comely wench rode past, bewigged, body-stockinged and chastely side-saddled. Neither was struck blind.

They would have been able to see across the road to Palace Yard, a handsomely gabled courtyard where Princess Elizabeth, daughter of James 1, had spent a night in November,

1605, to keep her out of reach of the Warwickshire-based Gunpowder Plotters beyond the city walls.

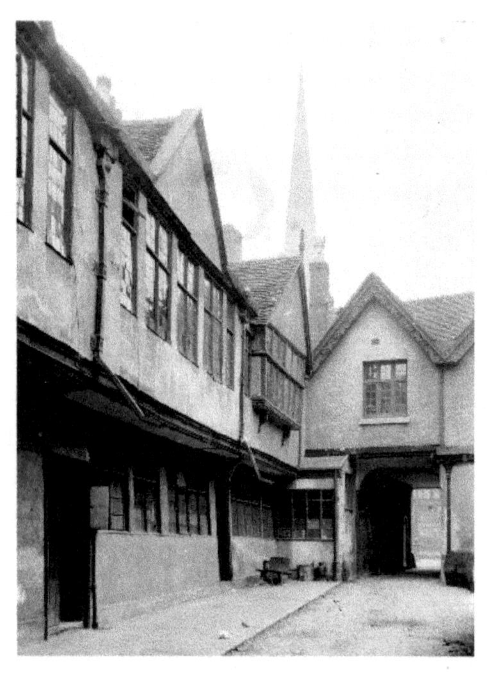

Palace Yard circa 1905 – not much different from how it would have looked in 1605 or November 13, 1940 (History Centre)

The Yard did not survive the blitz of 1940 – unlike a few of the elegant Georgian and Victorian buildings opposite, one of which has become yet another branch of Wetherspoon's.

Chance. Pure chance.

Nearby Christchurch, home of Coventry's third spire, also survived. Not for long, however. Almost 400 years after Henry VIII had ordered the original 14th century church and friary to be flattened, its early 19th century replacement was destroyed during one of the air raids that went on for four consecutive nights in April, 1941. But the spire still stood. Just about. It was badly cracked and, at one point, demolition had appeared to be the only option.

Thankfully, it didn't come to that. All three of the spires that had fascinated Turner and Tennyson remained aloft in Larkin's birthplace. Christchurch spire was, at a mere 211 feet, the smallest. It was also the oldest. Unlike the adjoining church and friary, it had survived the dissolution of the monasteries. In 1661, indeed, the spire and the three acres around it had been let out to Alderman Thomas Basnett, a prominent Parliamentarian in the English Civil War. Rent: £5 a year. Later the spire was used for keeping pigs by one Peter Seagar who apparently liked to boast that he had the highest sty in the world.

Is that a sty-in-the-sky story?

Certainly not. It came from an impeccable source: Peter Walters, no less, the author of two assiduously researched books on the city's history.

The shell of the church that had been rebuilt in the 1830s and destroyed by bombs in the 1940s was cleared away after the war. As a result, the spire was left somewhat marooned on what is now Dresden Place with the Methodist Central Hall on one side and a municipal car park on the other.

Today the spire houses a cafe-bar called, believe it or not, Inspires. Beer-lover, brewer and businessman Mick Leape set it up at the turn of the century after returning to his home city after a spell living in London and travelling the world. "It had briefly been a pottery shop and a blood bank," he confided during a brief break from brewing at the Twisted Barrel Brewery and Tap House at Fargo Village, a collection of offbeat shops, stalls, cafes and a gallery at the top end of Far Gosford Street. "I'd drunk quite a few monastic beers in Belgium," Mick continued, "so the spire attached to a former monastic church seemed an appropriate place to showcase them and show Coventrians that there was more to lager than Carling Black Label."

As for the space occupied originally by the mediaeval Church of the Grey Friars and then by the late-Georgian Christchurch, well that's being transformed into what might seem a somewhat surreal attachment to a 13th century spire. A new water park is set to open in the spring of 2019. With a 25-metre pool, since you ask. Plus slides, a spa, gym, dance studio and squash courts. The part backing on to the Inspires is already the size of a football stadium end.

Somehow I doubt that Larkin had a water park in mind when he posed the question in Church Going about what to do with religious buildings that fall out of use. But then he wrote that poem after a cycle ride through part of rural Northern Ireland in the 1950s. The centre of the city of his earlier life tends to be considerably busier. And that would have been true even in the late 1930s – particularly on Saturday afternoons when he would have walked past Christchurch en route to Hanson's music shop round the corner in Hertford Street.

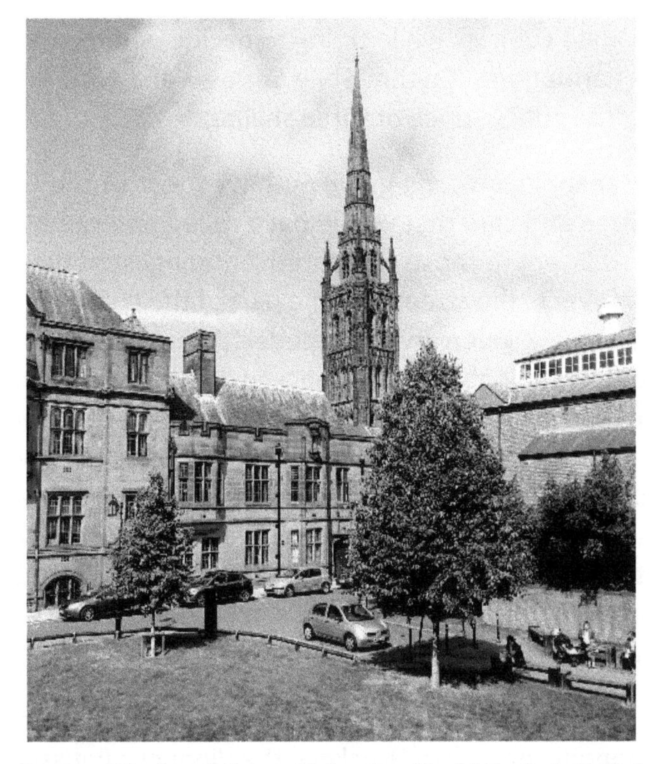

Frontage of the Council House with the spire of the "old" cathedral behind

By then he had begun to develop an ear for what would become a lifelong interest: jazz. Later in life, indeed, he would become the Daily Telegraph's jazz critic and give talks to the Hull Jazz Record Society at the White Hart pub. But he was still in his teens when, along with his friend Jim Sutton, he would thumb through the works of Louis Armstrong, Bix Beiderbecke, Sidney Bechet, Pee Wee Russell, and more of those who brought the music of the Mississippi to the Midlands of England at a speed of 78 revolutions per minute. In a piece called *Not the Place's Fault*, written for the Coventry Umbrella (arts) Club magazine in 1959, Larkin would later recall "frowning intently" in the shop's glass cubicles while trying to decide whether both sides of the Parlophone Rhythm-Style Series were good enough to justify "the stiffish price of three shillings".

Hanson's has long gone. So have most of the Coventry-built bikes and cars that would have rolled and rumbled along Hertford Street in those comparatively congested days. In the post-war years the street became part of the country's first city centre largely given over to pedestrians. Now one side of Hertford Street is about to be knocked down again, by bulldozers rather than bombs, as part of the latest redevelopment. But there are still traces of '30s red brick above the shops and restaurants on the side that wasn't completely blitzed in the 1940s. Larkin's haven of 78s would have been somewhere in the stretch now occupied by a typical 21st century Coventry mixture of a Chinese hairdresser's, a student letting agency, a nail bar and a British Heart Foundation charity shop.

Further along is a British Army recruiting office and a long-standing branch of Druckers, the Viennese Patisserie chain founded 20 miles or so up the road in Birmingham by Austrian emigre Andre Drucker.

Between all those creamy cakes and a branch of Poundland is something else typically Coventry: a passageway offering a framed view of Ford's Hospital, a handsome half-timbered building erected in 1509 as alms houses and still providing homes for elderly people to this day. Larkin would have known it, as well as another survivor still accessible between a newsagent and a legal firm round the corner in New Union Street. What is now the city's register office was once part of Cheylesmore Manor which dates back to the 13th century. Queen Isabella, widow of Edward II, and her grandson Edward, the Black Prince had dealings with it. So did Henry VI.

But the building had long passed out of royal hands when Sydney Larkin used to stride by it on his daily walk from Manor Road to the Council House. By that time, it had been plastered over. The original timber frame was only exposed after an extensive restoration by the City Council in the late 1960s.

As for Philip Larkin, he may well have sloped past Cheylesmore Manor on his way back to Manor Road after those Saturday-afternoon visits to the record shop. It's fair to say that Jim Sutton's step would have been considerably lighter as he set off for his own expansive family home in Beechwood Avenue, Earlsdon -- one of the city's more desirable addresses that, in parts, still has the aspect of a country lane to this day.

Young Philip made little secret of his envy of the Sutton spread with its tennis court, two garages, ornamental pond and, as he himself put it in Not the Place's Fault, "a spare room or two that could be given over to a Hornby lay-out or a miniature battlefield that need not be cleaned up by the end of the day". In the same article, he admitted to being "happy" at Chateau Sutton.

Larkin happy? In Coventry or anywhere else?

Almost unprecedented.

Mind you, his own family was not exactly shoe-horned in to Penvorn on the corner of Manor Road and St Patrick's Road. It was a substantial semi-detached with five-bedrooms, a drawing room, dining room, kitchen, hall and cellar. A decent-sized garden, too, surrounded by a privet hedge and accessed via French windows.

Not a matter of size then, this envy of young Philip's. It was more to do with sociability. There was what he himself called an "airy hospitality" about the Suttons. And that was something evidently lacking in the Larkin household by all accounts. Sutton himself talked about the place being "frightening" while another school friend, Colin Gunner, told the poet's biographer Andrew Motion, "If you put a speck on the floor, it was like spitting on the altar."

Tom Wilson, yet another friend, once told me about Philip's sixth birthday party. "He got a bit over-excited and was sent straight to bed. He was allowed down to blow out his candles, but it put a bit of a damper on proceedings, to put it mildly."

Now you might imagine that it was his Hitler-smitten father who imposed such rigid discipline. But in this particular instance you'd be wrong. It was his mother, Eva – "Mop" as opposed to "Pop", as Philip addressed his parents. The same Mop, that is, whom the poet would write to twice a week from Pop's death in 1948 until the mid-1970s. Except, that is, when mother and son briefly shared a house in Leicester during the late 1940s.

Philip Pullen has ploughed through mounds of those letters. Yes, that Philip Pullen – Coventrian and prominent member of the Philip Larkin Society, whom I met in the Royal Station Hotel in Hull. (On a busy weekday lunchtime rather than a hushed and melancholy Friday night that Larkin so memorably captured in his poem.) The same Philip Pullen, that is, who confirmed my suspicion that the poet's attitude to Coventry was as complex and contradictory as everything else about him.

Here's an example from Pullen's chapter on the Larkins in *Writers and their Mothers*, recently published by Palgrave Macmillan. "I think so often about our days in Coventry," the poet wrote to his mother in 1974, by which time she had evolved from Mop into Dearest Old Creature. "How the traffic used to go up and down St Patrick's Road, and I'd come home in the evening to find you 'picking fruit', with a cupful of water to put the maggots in – poor maggots! Do you remember how Daddy never liked hot pie, so his piece was always cut out and left to cool?"

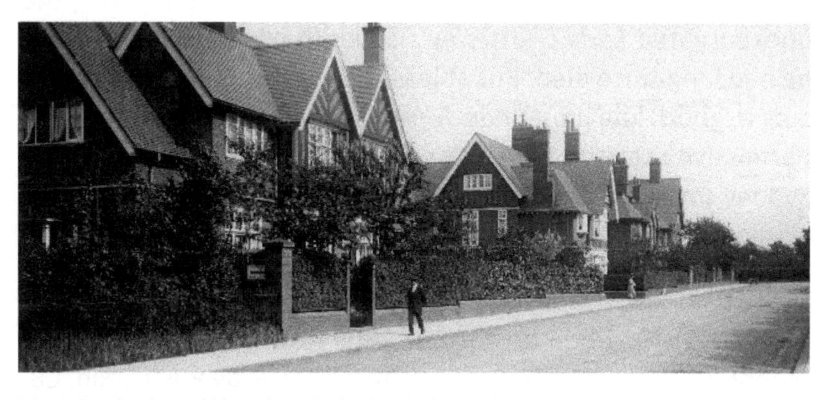

Manor Road as it would have been in the days before Sydney Larkin's favoured Fuhrer sent his Luftwaffe for a flying visit (Earlsdon Research Group)

Okay, it's not exactly Laurie Lee recalling his childhood in Slad. But in another piece, *Penvorn – a sense of place*, written for the Larkin Society magazine, Pullen quotes from another of the poet's letters to his mother, written in 1951. "And if I stopped to think, I can remember the rowanberries over the garage, the big plodding noise of station horses going by outside, and the light of the street lamp to the leaves on my bedroom." That article also has photographs of Philip playing cricket in the garden with one of his sister Kitty's friends keeping wicket, and of Eva relaxing in a deckchair with a book. There's a mention of the blossom that filled the garden in spring and of Sydney indulging in his pastime of bottling fruit for jam and cherry brandy.

Sydney's main pastime was reading. The drawing room was his domain and it was packed with books. He was particularly fond of the works of D H Lawrence. By the time of the great courtroom furore over Penguin's publication of the unexpurgated *Lady Chatterley's Lover* in paperback, however, he had long since died. But at least that attempted ban gave his son a good line in *Annus Mirabilis*, his ironic take on the permissive society of the '60s. And, whatever fears or miseries Sydney imposed on Philip, he passed on a love of books that would be the making of him as an Oxford graduate, a librarian and a poet.

By 1979, when he gave an interview by letter to his old school magazine *The Coventrian*, he was already P.A. Larkin, CB, MA, D.Lit, FRSL. Oh, yes, and D Litt again (Oxford rather than Warwick) with two 'ts'. Asked whether he had happy or unhappy memories of Coventry, the short answer could be summed up as both. "I was happy when I was at the Preparatory School and the first form of the main school . . . and then again in the sixth form," he reflected, "but in between I should say I was more unhappy than not. Perhaps it was an affair of being frightened rather than hurt, but one was hurt sometimes, and anyway being frightened is not very pleasant."

"Happy" at preparatory school?

In a letter to his mother written in 1952 he recalled being "rigid with fright" when "they hid my shoe-bag" and "Peter Snipe harried me all the way home".

To which "Mop" replied that she "never knew until now why your little nose and face always looked as though they had been rubbed in the dust each day when you came home. . . What a brave creature, you didn't even complain about it."

It could be argued that he made up for his lack of complaint over many years that followed. But in that interview for The Coventrian he went on to write, "I suppose the things I remember with most affection about Coventry are the old town around the cathedral (much of it now destroyed), watching football at Coundon Road [rugby football in other words], going to the Central Library in the evening to change books, and much further back being taken walks along lanes quite near where we lived on Manor Road, now long built over."

There's a picture of one of those lanes in Richard Bradford's book on Larkin the photographer, *The Importance of Elsewhere*. Philip and Eva are pictured in 1929 under a handsome sandstone railway bridge at the point where Coat of Arms Bridge Road runs into Stivichall Croft. Presumably the sepia photo was taken by Sydney or Kitty. Or was it by Philip himself? After all, the book's front cover shows him to have been an unlikely exponent of the "selfie" long before the advent of mobile phones.

Anyway, the bridge is still there, still engraved on either side with the coat of arms of the Gregory family, local lords of the manor, still carrying trains en route to and from Leamington. Still bordered, what's more, by open fields, ancient cottages, woodland and the vast expanse of the War Memorial Park. Yes, there are more houses than there would have been in Larkin's day. More traffic as well. But for all the industrial expansion that happened since the poet lived here, Coventry remains a surprisingly green city. That's a subject we shall return to in a future chapter.

While in Stivichall (or Styvechale as it's better known today), it's worth pointing out that just up the road and round the corner from the bridge is Amorial Road where Sydney stayed at the home of his deputy treasurer, Dr A. Marshall, in the days after the November blitz. It was a bit further out of the centre of town than Penvorn and considered marginally safer. Eva had already left for Litchfield before that fateful night for a brief stay with Sydney's relatives.

Philip Larkin hitch-hiked back to Coventry from Oxford soon after news of the city's devastation had spread. With him was fellow undergraduate and Coventrian Noel Hughes. They found Penvorn "relatively unscathed", according to Philip Pullen. "Having knocked on the door and received no answer, Hughes reckoned that Larkin didn't bother to ask any of the neighbours about his parents, and felt that was indicative of the fact that his family didn't know anybody nearby. But that's not true. He did go round asking the neighbours. I've seen it in his letters. It was another example of people's recollections of Larkin being a bit suspect. They tend to come from one angle or another."

For some reason or another, Sydney, Eva and Philip were all at the house on the night of April 8, 1941. This time slates were broken, plaster cracked and glass shattered by the bombing. Philip's "fear" must have returned with a vengeance on that occasion. But in a letter to Kitty the following day, he came over as comparatively blasé about it:

"Subsequent to my first air raid with real live bombs (last night) I am sound in mind and body. So is Pop and Mop who is here as well, but the general opinion prevailing at present is that you shouldn't return as you had intended."

Pop and Mop were in the process of moving to Warwick. As a prominent City Council employee, Sydney may have been aware of plans for an inner ring road that would take out the Larkins' end of Manor Road. The house was subject to a compulsory purchase order and went for £3,000. Philip made a brief visit from Oxford in 1943 and duly sent a letter to his parents reporting that he had "wandered morosely around the front garden, peering into the hall window". And found nothing much to report, apparently. No signs of life. Just some fire buckets and an extinguisher in the hall. "There were no indications that it was being used or that it was not being cared for," he added. "I slank away, expecting to be arrested."

He wasn't. As for the house, it became first a private rented residence and then a residential care home. The final demolition didn't come about until 1971. "So Penvorn has finally gone!" Larkin confirmed in another of his many letters to Eva. "Colin Gunner wrote to me to say that it has finally been knocked down. I expect it has. In a way, I should like to have given it one more look, as most of my memories are associated with it rather than any other house, but no doubt it would have been rather a sad business."

- According to Andrew Motion's biography of Larkin, *A Writer's Life*, he was approached by Blake Morrison to include the piece he wrote for the Umbrella Club in a collection of *Required Writing: Miscellaneous pieces (1955-1982)*. Politely but predictably, Larkin replied that he would prefer it "to remain in obscurity" on the grounds that it "exposes more of me than I want exposed".

CHAPTER 4

"Very fair" at School

Anybody retracing Sydney Larkin's walk to work 80 years on would have to start at a somewhat anachronistic little garden at the far end of one of Coventry's many blocks of student flats. Or should we call them a row of apartments in this case? They're certainly a cut above the average block. Those on the corner of Manor Road and Park Road have curved balconies overlooking the prospective new business quarter and the station. Not forgetting the preparatory school that young Philip attended. These days it's still a place for small children with parents able to fork out the fees to prepare them (eventually) for life at Bablake, the other former-grammar-turned-independent school in Coventry.

And that garden some hundred yards away from Philip's first school: was it once attached to Penvorn?

There's certainly a privet hedge in there somewhere, albeit severely cropped as well as dwarfed by a nearby monkey-puzzle tree. No fruit trees, mind you. No peace and quiet either. Not with 10 lanes of traffic thundering by below. Admittedly, four of those lanes are slip roads on to the ring road and Penvorn and its garden may be under one or, more likely, two of them. Who knows?

What I do know is that the wall separating the student apartments from that little public garden has a plaque attached to it. No, not a blue plaque pointing out that this is about as close as you're going to get to the house where one of the 20th century's finest poets lived for 13 years. It's an off-white white plaque with black lettering. "By order of Coventry City Council," it says, "Your alcoholic drink may be confiscated. You may be prosecuted for drinking alcohol in public in this area. Maximum penalty £500."

So there.

Coventry University students lucky enough to afford one of the Manor Road apartments above the site of his former family home would have to walk in a similar direction to Sydney Larkin – their place of study being a few hundred yards beyond what was once his place of work. Similar direction, very dissimilar surroundings.

A footbridge has long been required to get from Manor Road to what remains of Friar's Road, separated as they are by the aforesaid ring road.

Is it noisy up there?

Pardon?

IS IT NOISY UP THERE?

You bet it is.

And having traversed those 10 lanes, what's the first thing you see?

Yet another crane hovering over yet another site of prospective student apartments. As for the rest of Friar's Road, most of the houses that would have been fairly new in the 1930s are nearly all "student lets", as the signs outside proclaim.

By now you may well be asking why we're retracing Sydney's brisk walk to work rather than Philip's trudge to school.

Well, there is a somewhat tenuous and slightly fuggy connection in the form of an old-fashioned tobacconist's. It's called Salt's and since 1961 it has stood across the street from the far end of Friars Road, on the corner of what is now "New" Union Street and Little Park Street. No, it wouldn't have been there in Sydney's day but it remains the sort of place that he would have recognised. So would Philip as an avid collector of cigarette cards in his childhood days and an inveterate smoker as an adult.

Salt's is very much a man's shop. The window harbours pipes and cigar cutters, silver cigarette cases and shaving brushes. Even the odd bottle of single malt.

Brazenly on display inside are packets of cigarettes – Peterson and Players, Condor and Craven A – at prices that would have bought a lifetime's supply of Havana cigars rolled on a virgin's thigh in the days when the Larkins lived in Coventry. Each packet is taped with a message in large, bold lettering: "SMOKING KILLS."

The current owner, Pat Henry, took on the shop from his father-in-law over 40 years ago. Did he feel any guilt about selling a product considered so detrimental to health?

"Standing behind a Corporation bus does much the same," he shrugged.

And did he smoke himself?

"The occasional small cigar."

Philip Larkin liked more than the occasional cigarette, it would seem. He used to savour a menthol fag with his gin and tonic, according to James Booth, the most recent of his biographers. And, as Philip Pullen of the Philip Larkin Society reminded me, "you can see him smoking nonchalantly, and apparently enjoying doing so, while being interviewed by [John] Betjeman for the BBC's Monitor programme". That took place at Larkin's home in Hull in 1964 when warnings about the damaging effects of tobacco were still in their infancy.

Just about every adult smoked during his own infancy, childhood and adolescence in pre-war Coventry. Gutters would have been strewn with nub-ends as well as another bi-product of those packets of Players, Park Drive and Woodbines. Larkin revealed what it was in the 1959 article that he wrote for the Umbrella Club magazine when he reminisced about his walk from Manor Road to Henry VIII School on nearby Warwick Road:

"I sometimes think the slight scholarly stoop in my bearing today was acquired by looking for cigarette cards in Coventry gutters. There seemed to be a 'Famous Cricketers' series every summer then."

He went on to list some of those fabled names whose cards he coveted, including [Frank] Woolley, A.W. Carr, R.E.S. Wyatt ("who went to my school"), [Les] Ames and [Wally] Hammond. (In those days the English game was divided between Gentlemen and Players, and only the gents were granted the courtesy of initials before their names.)

There was, Larkin recalled, a cigarette machine next to the newspaper seller outside the station. Apparently it "gave ten cigarettes for sixpence and twenty for a shilling (but with the twenty you got a halfpenny back under the cellophane)". The poet went on to admit that one of his fantasies was to unlock the machine "and rifle the packets for cigarette cards".

Earlier In the same paragraph he recalled some other aspects of his walk to and from school. "Coming up the short, somehow rather unofficial road that joins Warwick Road by the Station Hotel took me past the station horses in their carts outside the Goods Office. When I went back at lunchtime they were wearing their nosebags, and on my return at a quarter to two there was a scatter of chaff on the ground where they had stood. I liked this corner best at summer teatime, where in addition to the man selling the Midland Daily Telegraph, there was frequently a white Eldorado box-tricycle that sold lime green or strawberry-pink ices at a penny each."

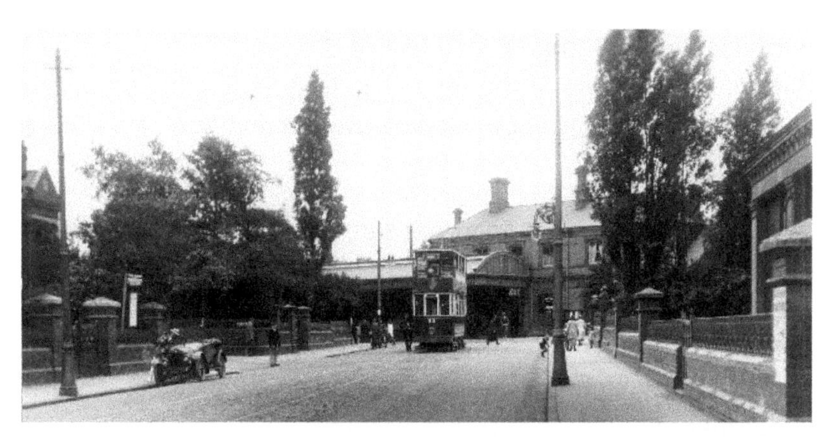

The frontage of Coventry Station that young Philip passed en route to school
(Earlsdon Research Group)

Ice-cream sellers are about as rare as horses and fag machines outside the station today. In fact, the only place selling cigarettes is the W H Smith's outlet on the main concourse. You can see the packets peeping from behind two black sliding doors near the till. Strictly for sale to over-18s, says a sign alongside the usual warnings about imminent death for those who persist with lighting up. Not that you'd be allowed to light up in the shop, nor in any of the offices or coffee bars hereabouts. Smoking indoors has long been banned, needless to say.

And, needless to say, there are no nose-bagged horses beyond the concourse. Instead there are lines of taxis of the sort that south-bound passengers will also find as soon as they step out on to the Euston Road or head for the cab-rank. So-called London black cabs have long been made in Coventry. And still are, even if the London Taxi Company is now Chinese-owned.

Coventry, incidentally, was the first city to be linked to London by train. Hence George Eliot's use of the fear of the coming of the railway as a one of the themes in Middlemarch; and hence Tennyson fantasising about Godiva while changing trains as long ago as 1840.

A station first opened here in 1838, although it wasn't much more than a halt on the line that would eventually connect London with Birmingham. Only pressure from the local ribbon manufacturers brought about an increase in size to a proper station from which their products could be exported to a much wider market.

That station was still standing (just about) when Larkin pulled in shortly before writing I Remember, I Remember – although the building that he would have remembered so well had been badly damaged in one bombing raid or another. Still, a replacement was on its way. The new station opened in 1962, in uncompromisingly modernist style, and twice the size of its predecessor. Yes, the roof remains a great concrete slab, but there's a wooden ceiling beneath it and the walls are almost entirely glass, bestowing brightness on the concourse on the dullest of days. Plans are now afoot to redevelop the station in what might be termed post-modernist style.

Beyond the front entrance, buses pull in over a short patch of well-worn cobbles that would have been there in Larkin's day and beyond. And, as in his day, you can cut through past the site of the Station Hotel that later became the Rocket pub, once a haven for Coventry City supporters en route to away matches and to members of The Specials, The Selecter, The Beat and Madness in the days when 2-Tone music was in its prime and the Horizon Studios were across the road. The pub was demolished a few years ago and remains a potential building site – one of quite a few in this part of town.

As I mentioned in an earlier chapter, you can no longer see all three spires from the bridge where Tennyson fantasised about Godiva. But glance to the left up Warwick Road and clearly outlined against the skyline are the castellated turrets of Larkin's former school.

Close up, the building looks even more impressive, designed as it was in the era of high Victorian pomp by one E.

Burgess of London. The red brick is overlaid here and there with elaborate stonework; the chimneys are worthy of Lutyens and there's a central square tower below which is a handsome stone engraving of the coat of arms of Henry VIII. Well, the recently restored "Old Grammar School" on the corner of Hales Street, which we gazed at from the Philip Larkin pub in Chapter One, was named after him. Just as Hales Street was named after the school's founder, John Hales.

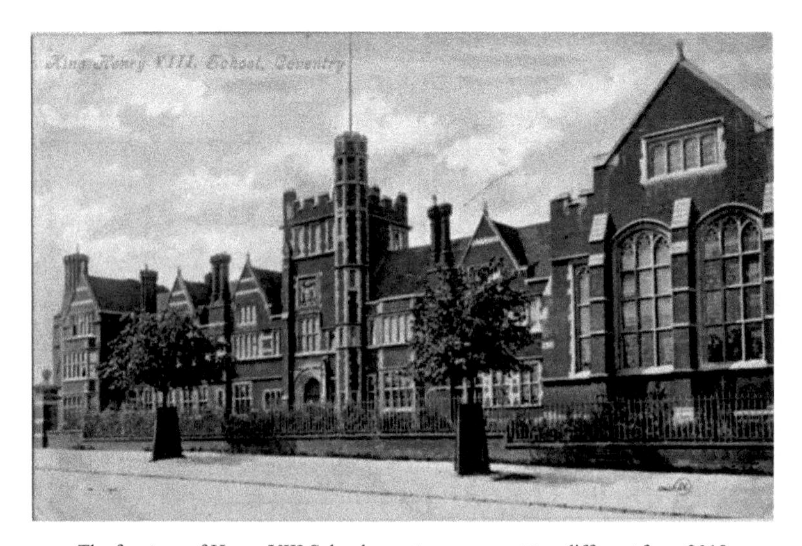

The frontage of Henry VIII School a century ago - not too different from 2018
(Earlsdon Research Group)

Fees today amount to £11,352 for a school year, although the Coventry School Foundation provides bursaries to around a third of pupils. "Henry's", as it has always been known locally, was a boys-only grammar school in Larkin's day. He was here from 1930 until 1940, as a gleaming plaque to his memory reminds us in the entrance hall.

No blue plaque yet on that opulent frontage, but it's a start. The frontage, incidentally, had to be much restored in the wake of the bombing of April, 1941. Near the plaque is a photograph of the devastated entrance hall as it was soon after the Luftwaffe left for their beloved homeland. Pupils had long been evacuated by then and Larkin was already at Oxford, of course. It was left to his former head teacher A.A.C. Burton and his staff to clear up the remains of a building that had almost gone for a Burton.

As they rummaged through the rubble, the head was particularly keen to find his "punishment book". In it was a list of lashings and lines administered to the boys in his care. Larkin featured four times. Lines rather than lashings in his case. Which must have been extremely tedious for one who was already bent on turning language into poetry rather than a repetitive dictum. His first poem had been published in the school magazine, The Coventrian, when he was 11. "He evidently hadn't done anything serious enough to warrant the cane or the strap" I was assured by Don Lee, one-time lecturer at the WEA (Workers' Education Association) and the creator of a Larkin Trail around Coventry that I remember, I remember following some 20 years ago.

We shall be dipping into Don's prodigious knowledge of Larkin later. For now we have an appointment with two other experts on the poet's words and deeds during his days at Henry's.

Former head of English Sheila Woolf and current librarian and archivist Helen Cooper were waiting for me behind a glass door at the far end of the school library where a sepulchral silence reigned as pupils bent diligently over computer screens surrounded by books.

There were plenty more books in the Larkin Room which Ms Woolf – Sheila to you and me – set up in 2002, exactly 80 years after the poet's birth. That room will be stuffed with "Larkinalia" nearly 100 years on when Coventry takes the City of Culture crown from Hull. "The Brynmor Jones Library [Larkin's lair at Hull University] is going to lend us artefacts from their exhibition so that we can have one here," she confided.

Helen, meanwhile, had dug out a veritable treasure-trove of young Philip's school reports. It's fair to say that the word "fair" features frequently. "Very fair" in some cases. "Only fair" in mathematics in July, 1933, which was a slight advance on the end of the previous term: "Rather slow". By the end of the following school year his art teacher was more expansive than most. "Term work poor; can do better," was his verdict.

And Sheila's verdict?

"He was mainly interested in English. Only when he settled down to the sixth-form did he become a good scholar."

As if to emphasise that point, Helen had truffled out a letter from the head, A.A.C. Burton (M.A. Oxon), dated October 26, 1943, to P.A. Larkin, Esq., who had just become a BA Oxon. With a first-class degree in English from St John's College. In response to Larkin's request for a reference, Burton expressed no surprise at his university success – "for he was undoubtedly the most brilliant English scholar that we have had in my time here".

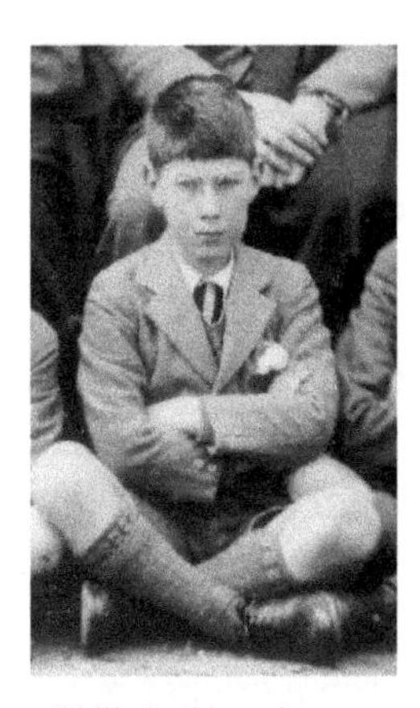
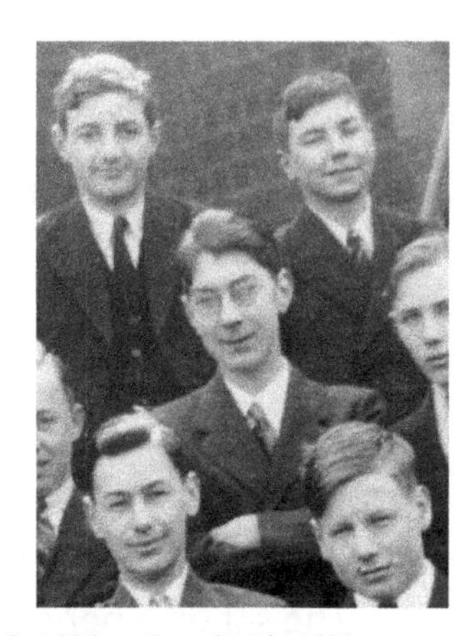

Philip Larkin as he was aged 12, in 1934, and aged 16 in 1938
(Henry VIII School)

As for the most brilliant cricketer that Henry's ever produced, that accolade would go to former Warwickshire and England captain R.E.S. Wyatt. His return to the school to give a talk in 1933 ended with him being swamped by autograph hunters, 11-year-old Philip Larkin among them. "He loved cricket," Sheila confirmed. More as a spectator than a player, it would seem.

At which point she showed me a letter written by P.A. Larkin of the Brynmor Jones Library, Hull, on May 16, 1985, shortly before his death. It was addressed to "Ms Woolf" to thank her for sending him three copies of the Coventrian. They evidently brought back some sylvan memories of matches past, judging by the way he could identify so many team members and umpires in a photograph of a match between the School and Old Boys at the end of one summer term.

He was even more expansive in an article published in the same school magazine not too long after his death, with the kind permission of the Philip Larkin estate. It was evidently written sometime in the previous decade when he had an engagement near Coventry and, to use his own words "was moved" to visit the place where he was born and had spent the first 18 years of his life.

Larkin had evidently learnt to drive by the time the piece was written and found himself pleasantly surprised while heading towards his old school, up Spencer Avenue in Earlsdon – "not because things were different, but because they were the same". Might have been 1939, apparently. He goes on to describe how he sat on a bench to watch a cricket match on the playing fields, reminiscing about matches past, his own ineptitude as a player and the tuck-shop staying open to provide Chelsea buns and ginger beer. The last sentence is an evocation of the timeless beauties of the game in a place that evidently brought back warm memories as the sun sank behind the trees and the shadows lengthened.

That cricket pitch is still there today. And there are still nets and covers and sightscreens and a rather handsome, traditional scoreboard with a redbrick surround and a tiled roof. Admittedly some newish outbuildings have been tagged on to the school since Larkin's last visit, and the twee roofs of Next, Outfit, Boots and other familiar names peep above the dip that houses the Central Six Retail Park. But this is still posh Cov. Wide-open spaces. Big houses. The substantial six-bedroomed semi just across the green from the school was recently on the market for around £650,000.

Stroll past the school on a summer Saturday afternoon and there is almost invariably a match taking place, both teams in immaculate whites. Turn right past the lawns and flower beds of Top Green and stroll on to the much wider open spaces of the War Memorial Park, however, and the majority of kids will be panting and sweating over impromptu football matches. Cricket is no longer played in most state schools and interest in the game has declined accordingly. Except, that is, in Asian communities where an engaging passion for the game is still nurtured outside school.

We shall be returning to the enormous Memorial Park in the next chapter. It covers 48.5 hectares (not far off 120 acres in real money) and was opened in July, 1921, to commemorate the 2,587 Coventrians who died in the so-called "war to end all wars". That was just over a year before the birth of Philip Larkin and just over 18 years before the outbreak of the next world war.

CHAPTER 5

Caught Smoking on a Grave

The title is MCMXIV, which I'm sure the Latin scholars among you will instantly translate to 1914. But it's not the title that sticks in the memory. With the notable exception of This Be The Verse, it's Larkin's last lines that linger. "Never such innocence again," in this case.

Loss would have been all too evident in the Coventry that he grew up in. Not just loss of innocence but loss of limbs, loss of hearing, loss of minds. And, it almost goes without saying, loss of lives. Widows would have been plentiful, many of them struggling to hold back tears at sensitive moments. Some women were destined to stay single as able-bodied men were in short supply, for a while at least. Lost fiancés. Lost boyfriends.

Lives lost amounted to well over two and a half thousand in this city alone, as mentioned at the end of the last chapter. Some 450 copper beech trees had been planted in the Memorial Park by 1923. They would have been little more than saplings during Larkin's childhood. Nearly 250 of them were dedicated to those men whose families could shell out 25 shillings (£1.25) for a plaque to place at their roots. There would be more plaques to come. Many more.

Field Marshal Douglas Haig, no less, turned up to dedicate the war memorial itself – 90ft high, white and handsomely decorative – on October 8th, 1927. Alongside him was a mere Corporal, one Arthur Hutt, a Coventry-born winner of the

Victoria Cross in the so-called "Great War". A local woman was also prominent in proceedings. Eliza Bench from Foleshill had lost four sons in the carnage on the Western Front. Her grieving husband was not allowed to accompany her. Only one representative of each family was permitted to join the ceremony.

Whether five-year-old Philip Larkin was among the spectators is a matter of conjecture. What's more certain is that he would have known the park reasonably well as time went on. Apart from anything else, the sports areas were used by his school as overspill from its own playing fields. And although Philip was taken by Sydney to watch Coventry RFC play at their original ground on Coundon Road, it's difficult to imagine him relishing being in a scrum or indeed standing in the three-quarter line keenly waiting to be set loose by the fly half.

Don Lee has as one of the entries in his Larkin trail the churchyard of St James's in Styvechale where the teenage Philip was found playing truant from rugby and "lounging across a gravestone smoking" before being "summarily ejected".

The appeal of that churchyard was all too evident some 80 years on. It just happened to be a glorious day in May when I paid a visit and a gnarled and ancient yew tree was bedecked by an abundance of bluebells with a solitary red tulip protruding from their midst. Not even the traffic passing by on the nearby Leamington Road could disturb the sense of peace and unexpected beauty.

No, I wasn't going to launch into Gray's Elegy. This was not a country churchyard after all. It happens to be well within the boundaries of a city harbouring not only swathes and nooks of natural beauty but a surprising literary heritage. Just down the road and round the corner from the spot where young Larkin was ejected for a grave offence is Salisbury Avenue where the knell of parting life tolled for E M Forster.

Yes, the author of, among others, Passage to India and Howards End – novels that more than likely graced the crammed shelves of Sydney Larkin's drawing room.

Forster had an apartment at Brunswick Square in Bloomsbury and enjoyed a lengthy association with King's College, Cambridge. So how on earth did he end his days on a road of bow and bay-windowed semis in suburban Coventry?

Let's call it "the love that dare not speak its name". That's what they did call it in some quarters until 1967 when homosexuality was finally legalised for adults over 21. Forster was getting on a bit by that time. Well into his 80s, in fact. He died three years later, aged 91, on 7 June, 1970, as it says on a plaque over a garage at the bottom end of Salisbury Avenue.

This was once the home of Bob and May Buckingham. Bob had been a "bobby" in London before joining the Coventry police force. He had met Forster some years previously at the Oxford and Cambridge boat race. Not surprisingly, May was far from happy when she discovered their affair. Yet she mellowed over the years and, rather touchingly, she acted as nursemaid to the author in his later years. In May, 1970, she and Bob fetched him from his rooms in King's College following his final stroke, and put him to bed at their home where she was holding his hand at the end. Later she wrote about their initial stormy relationship and how, "over the years he changed us both and he [Forster] and I came to love one another, able to share the joys and sorrows that came".

Sounds like a good example of the author's mantra, which is now better known as the title of a TV quiz show. Larkin was only too well aware of it, having read it first in Howards End. Jean Hartley, co-publisher of The Less Deceived and The Whitsun Weddings, once told me that she, Philip and her husband George used to go to boxing matches at the City Hall in Hull. On one occasion the fighters were circling one another, feinting this way and that for what seemed an eternity. At which point the librarian and poet was heard to mutter "only connect".

The house where Forster finally lost connection with the Buckinghams and the wider world is now owned by Kevin and Celia Williams, who were happy to show me not only the plaque over their garage but a framed tribute to the author in their hall. It's signed by "friends and admirers" from King's College, including Sir Michael and Lady Faith Culme-Seymour.

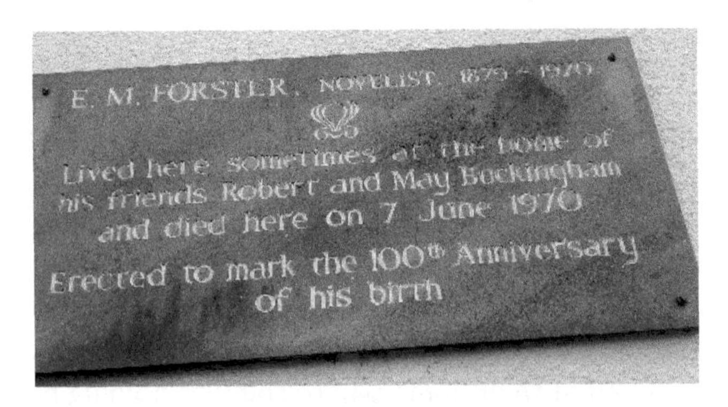

Plaque marking the death-place of E.M. Forster

"How much do you think I'd get for that on eBay?" grinned Kevin, a genial former miner who now works in a foundry.

"He's joking," Celia assured me before leading the way through their handsomely extended kitchen to a window overlooking the garden. A room with a view, you might say. "His [Forster's] ashes are out there by the rose bushes," she pointed out before digging out a book on E M Forster and His World by Francis King. And there it was in black and white: "After Forster's death . . . his ashes were scattered over a rose bush in the Buckinghams' garden, where they were later joined by those of Bob Buckingham."

Coventry has never made much of its literary heritage. Its road signs once carried the rather lame claim that it was "the city in Shakespeare country". Neighbouring Nuneaton has a statue to George Eliot in the town centre and a permanent exhibition about her life, times and local connections in its museum and art gallery. Yet one of the great English novelists of the 19th century, and indeed of all time, spent her formative years in the city down the road where the imposing house she grew up in has been allowed to go to rack and ruin. The city, that is, where one of the most highly regarded novelists of the early 20th century spent much of his later life and uttered his final words. The city, that is, where one of the great poets of the 20th century was born and brought up.

Now where did we leave him last?

Being chased out of St James's churchyard, you may recall. Getting back across the Leamington Road to the Memorial Park takes longer now than it would have done in his day because of the volume of traffic. Worth it, mind you, and not just for the sheer scale of the place – green as far as the eye can see. The many saplings from Larkin's day have, needless to say, matured and spread and been added to in the wake of the Second World War. This time Field Marshall Viscount Montgomery of El Alamein, otherwise known as "Monty", turned up and some 2,017 names were added to the Roll of Honour. Tellingly, 1,085 of them were civilians.

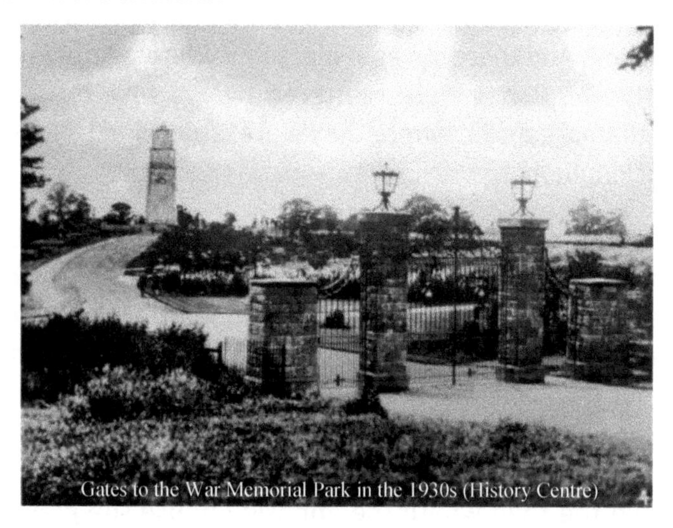
Gates to the War Memorial Park in the 1930s (History Centre)

Now there are more saplings to replace trees that have either withered with time or been damaged by extreme weather conditions.

Near the much-improved children's play area is a delightful pond, bordered by reeds and shrouded by shrubs and exotic trees. And near the tennis courts is a pillared pavilion. It was empty in the 1980s when I used to chase my children around it in games of "tig". Now it houses, among other things, a bustling coffee bar. Sometimes I find myself queuing behind someone who has just ordered three lattes, a bacon batch and a slice of chocolate fudge cake. Still, there are plenty of picnic benches outside where, eventually, I can savour an Americano while one or another of my grandkids sucks an ice lolly or slurps a hot chocolate.

There's another coffee bar in the middle distance, beyond the lower slopes of the football pitches and wild flower beds. It's on the side of a suitably decorous white building that came into being sometime between 2010 and 2013 when the park was upgraded with the help of a grant from the National Lottery. Now it has Green Flag status, granted only to the best green spaces. Grade II listed, what's more.

Inside that newish white building is not only an information desk but many moving tributes to "The Fallen". Some have sepia photographs alongside. Or black and white in the case of Montague Johnson, a talented violinist from nearby Spon End, pictured in full evening dress. Private Johnson was 21 when he died on the Somme on September 3rd, 1916. His commemorative plaque, otherwise known as a "Dead Man's Penny", was discovered in 1963 in a garden shed in Allesley, on the north-western edge of Coventry. It was Kim Kenny who found that "penny". She was five at the time.

Fifty three years later she brought it back to the Coventry from her home in Gloucester on the hundredth anniversary of Private Johnson's death. Montague's Song, a requiem to his memory, was created by composer/violinist Derek Nisbet of the Talking Birds theatre group and playwright Chris O'Connell of Theatre Absolute. This time it was performed not in the Shop Front Theatre (see Chapter One) but at St John the Baptist Church in nearby Fleet Street.

Montague's name now appears on a stained-glass window in St John's – the building which, coincidentally, played its part in what you might call a well-known phrase or saying. It was here that royalist prisoners were incarcerated during the English Civil War. This being a staunchly parliamentarian city, those prisoners were given the cold shoulder. Hence the term "sent to Coventry".

And Montague's story from the First World War?

"By a strange coincidence we found out that Derek was living two doors away from the house where the other violinist had lived before going off to fight in France," Chris O'Connell recalled. "But it was seeing that photograph and story about him in the Memorial Park that first sparked our interest."

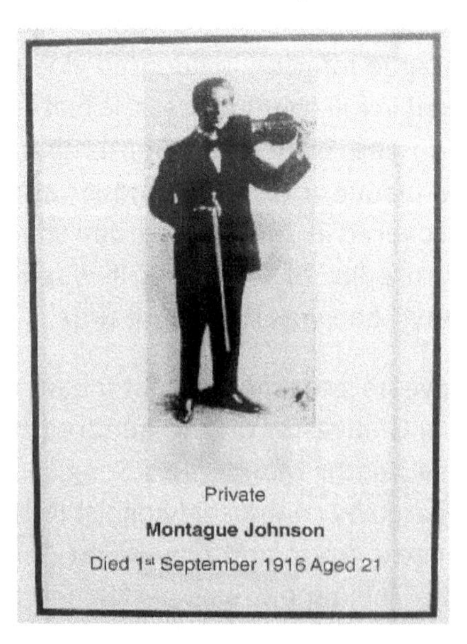

Private Montague Johnson, as remembered in the Memorial Park

The park would have been a somewhat staid and sombre place in Larkin's day, school rugby matches apart.

A century on from the end of the First World War, it still puts on a respectful ceremony on Remembrance Day when the Chamber of Silence with its Roll of the Fallen is opened inside the memorial itself. But silence is none too prevalent in the park during the Godiva Festival, the most recent manifestation of the Godiva procession and carnival that Larkin and his father used to leer over from the Council House balcony. Amplified rock bands can be sung along with in the back gardens of Styvechale and Earlsdon during those days and nights when the park is packed, crowds are flowing from one marquee to another and the fairground lights are swirling long into the night. The BBC's Big Weekend in May, 2018 , attracted revellers from far and wide. Liam Gallagher headed a bill that included the Stereophonics, Snow Patrol, UB40 and, on their home ground, The Selecter. Nigel Kennedy was even allowed in to perform on the Bank Holiday Monday, despite being a fervent Aston Villa supporter.

Now, perhaps, it's time to bid farewell to Memorial Park and cover the final few hundred yards of the lengthy trek from Leamington Road to luxuriously leafy Kenilworth Road.

Larkin used to cycle home along here in his late teens, slurring out an old blues song called See the Spider Climb that Wall at the top of his voice. By then he'd had a pint or three. "He used to go visiting pubs in Kenilworth with his friends," Don Lee had told me.

The singing poet would have pedalled past imposing houses with long tree-lined drives at the Kenilworth end of the road before crossing the A45 with signposts to London one way and Birmingham the other. To Larkin's right was, and still is, the stretch known as Kenpas Highway. And half a mile or so along there was the Kenpas open-air swimming pool where Henry VIII School used to stage inter-house swimming competitions. Even in high summer the water temperature apparently ranged from freezing to just about bearable.

That helps to explain his comment in a letter to Jim Sutton, written in 1950, when Larkin was a librarian in Wellington, Shropshire, and was engaged to one Ruth Bowman. The prospect of matrimony was to him "like going in first time at the Kenpas".

He couldn't go through with it. Not with Ruth, not with anybody. Not that he was short of women in his later days. Maeve Brennan and Monica Jones were the better known names on a lengthy list of lovers, including one Winifred Arnott. No relation, I might add, as I am from that rarer breed of Arnots with one "t". Larkin's biographers have discussed his relationships at some lengths and they're not really the subject of this book.

During his days in Coventry he never seemed to be short of friends. But they were all male. The only women in his life were his mother Eva and sister Kitty. Henry's in those days was an all-male environment. Girls weren't allowed in until the '70s. When informed about it in a letter from Jeff Vent OBE, long-time modern languages teacher who ran the Old Coventrians Association, the response was all too typical:

"How awful about the girls! My sister went to Barr's Hill [then the girls' grammar school in Coventry], but even that doesn't console me. I see the First XV has had a splendid record this season. . . " [quoted by Philip Pullen in a speech to the Larkin Symposium at Henry VIII School on December 2nd, 2015].

The old Kenpas pool closed many years ago and is now covered by a row of bungalows in what is known as Poolside Gardens.

As for Kenilworth Road, an American soldier stationed nearby allegedly described it as "a 64-thousand-dollar entrance to a 10-cent city". But then he would have been posted here shortly after the mediaeval heart of Coventry had been blitzed.

Today the road down which a beer-filled Philip cycled home from the pub(s) still displays long stretches of grass and woodland. They run all the way from the narrow band of farmland that separates the borders of Kenilworth and Coventry to the gateway to Warwick University and beyond. All the way indeed to his old school.

By no means all the woodland along both sides of the road is privately owned. Those of us lucky enough to live in Earlsdon can stroll out on a summer's evening and pick our way along pathways between ancient trees. The only intruder on this rural revel is the sound of traffic from the nearby main road. Much more of it, needless to say, than in Larkin's cycling days.

At this stage it's worth pointing out that the extensive stretches of greenery within Coventry are by no means confined to

Earlsdon and Styvechale. The soon-to-be-renovated mediaeval Charterhouse is surrounded by some 70 acres of common land. And that's just one of the many green spaces on the east side of town.

The hauntingly evocative London Road Cemetery, designed by Joseph Paxton and opened in 1847, stretches over 42 acres, houses a mass grave for victims of the blitz and a non-conformist chapel built like a classical temple. Not even the 9.43 thundering through on what is now the West Coast Main Line can disturb the special atmosphere of the place for long. (The railway to London, immortalised by George Eliot and Alfred Lord Tennyson, was laid down even earlier than the first coffin in the cemetery.)

Nearby is the main Binley Road where no sooner does Gosford Green peter out into a busy traffic island than Stoke Green appears on the other side. The five-fingered leaves of its splendid horse-chestnut trees seem to be weighing white candles in early summer and carrying ripening conkers thereafter. Nearby is an orchard. Further on is a cricket ground; then another vast green spread to the right. Horses are grazing in an open field towards the far end as you bear left towards Coombe Park – 500 acres of lakeside and woodland walks with formal gardens designed by Capability Brown. Okay, the park is just beyond the city borders but it's still owned by the City Council and open to city dwellers.

On the north-western edge of Coventry there's Coundon Wedge, offering the chance to stroll or stride to nearby Allesley through delightfully undulating pastures with a tree-lined brook, untrimmed hedges, buttercups and blackberries a-plenty in summer.

Much closer to the centre of a city written off by some as a "concrete jungle" is a lengthy dual carriageway down which I drive en route to Coundon to see my dentist or accountant, sometimes with comparable levels of trepidation. Over to the left the houses suddenly give way to another extensive spread of common land that seems to go on as far as the eye can see. It's called Lake View Park, although the lake never materialised. There is a nature reserve, however, and a good, visible stretch of the elusive River Sherbourne.

The artist George Shaw, shortlisted for the Turner Prize in 2011 and granted a solo exhibition at the National Gallery five years later, grew up on the city's Tile Hill estate. He once told me that he has carried it around in his head ever since. Whenever he paints a derelict pub or social club, the back of some empty garages or a grey block of concrete council flats, they are invariably encroached upon by the woodland that still surrounds the estate to this day. Could be anywhere in England, mind you. As the artist's fellow Coventrian put it at the end of I Remember, I Remember, "Nothing, like something, happens anywhere."

And to quote George Shaw directly from a piece I wrote for the Society section of the Guardian in 2003, "I like the idea that this place [Tile Hill] was carved out of the Forest of Arden."

Shakespeare's forest, in other words – the same forest, needless to say, that lines the Kenilworth Road on the south-west side of the city. Whether or not he was seeking what the Bard would call "a muse to ascend the brightest heaven of invention", Larkin would almost certainly have strolled through that part of the forest that links Kenilworth Road to Beechwood Avenue, Earlsdon, where Jim Sutton's parents had their extensive pile and the otherwise lugubrious would-be poet proclaimed himself to be "happy".

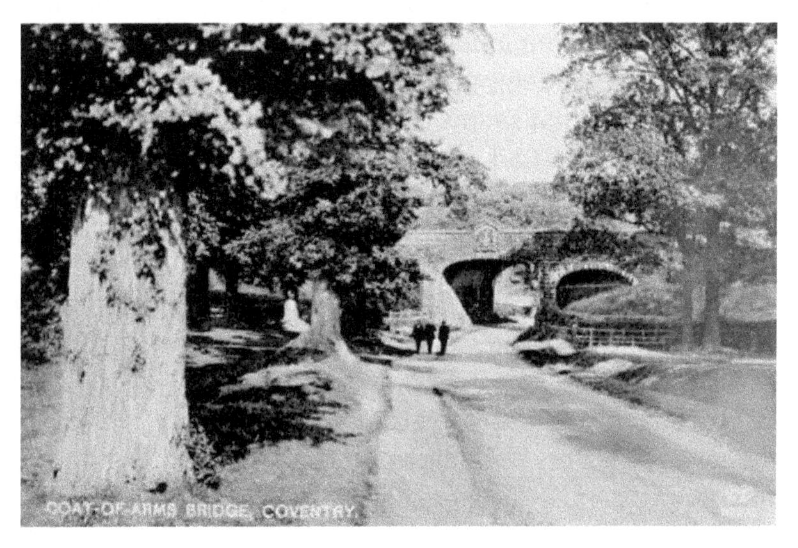

The bridge at Stivichall Croft is still surrounded by grass and trees nearly a century on from Larkin's childhood (Earlsdon Research Group)

This pathway to his childhood heaven begins not far from the railway bridge under which young Philip was photographed with his mother in 1929. On a May afternoon nearly 90 years on, the sign for the narrow entrance to Canley Ford was almost obliterated by dock leaves and dandelions. The sides of the narrow lane were frothing with cow parsley and the rumble of traffic was gradually replaced by birdsong. Bluebells spread to right and left beneath ancient elms and oaks, beech trees and birches. There were little pathways into the trees and then, to the left, a rustic gate leading to a meadow strewn with wild flowers and sloping down to the ford itself.

This could have been rural Kent; or Sussex; or anywhere in rural Middle England. Yet the city centre was only a couple of miles away and the four-lane highway leading to London one way and Birmingham the other would appear some way beyond the ford. Eventually.

I wasn't heading for the A45, so I circled back on the country lane towards Earlsdon where there was a sudden narrowing of perspective. The lane became a path that passed between thick hedges and then green railings with a golf course on either side. A grounds-man mowing one of the greens was only the fourth person I'd seen since I set off on this delightful rural ramble in the city. The other three were dog-walkers.

Eventually I emerged on to what seemed like the broad expanse of Bates Road. In Larkin's day it would have been just another rustic lane. Now it was dotted with post-war housing, mainly expansive bungalows. To left and right were little by-ways, one of which was enticingly labelled Nightingale Lane. But I was bound for the top of Bates Road. It finally emerged into Beechwood Avenue and there on the left was the former Chateau Sutton, now divided into two substantial semis.

It was time to do a bit of old-fashioned journalistic door-knocking.

CHAPTER 6

Stole a Book from the Library

Satvinder Singh opened the front door immediately and held up a friendly hand. "Could you just hang on a minute," he mouthed before carrying on talking into the phone in his other hand. For quite a long time, as it turned out.

No matter.

The view down Beechwood Avenue from the driveway of the house where Larkin revealed that he was "happy" in childhood was as pleasantly rustic as any in suburban Coventry. Particularly so on a glorious day in May with mature trees in full leaf and the verges beneath a-bloom with wild flowers. Birdsong mingled with the thwack of balls from the tennis club just behind those trees, next door to the golf course which I'd passed through en route from Canley Ford.

To my left was St Barbara's Church, consecrated in 1931 when Larkin and his chum Jim Sutton would have still been playing with Hornby train sets or toy soldiers in one of the many spacious rooms here at number 127. Sutton senior was a prosperous builder and no expense had been spared on what was then a detached family home, lovingly assembled towards the end of the 1920s with a garden that seemed to go on forever.

The door opened again. Satvinder was beckoning me towards the Singh side of the two semis that the former detached house now comprises. His apology for being so lengthily detained on a business call was unnecessary. Like his wife Siew, he was an insurance actuary by trade and you'd need to do a fair bit of trading to pay the insurance on this place, let alone the mortgage. It may have been half the size that it was in Larkin's childhood but there was still an air of grandeur about it, as I discovered after agreeing to remove my shoes before embarking on a guided tour.

Here and there were survivors of an earlier era. A stained-glass window glinted beneath a carved stairway. The original front windows were bowed and leaded. "They're coming out soon," Satvinder confided. "The wood's rotting."

There was still a carved arch on the landing outside the long, wide loft that now houses a luxurious en-suite guest bedroom. With a panoramic view, what's more, over a gently sloping predominantly green landscape. Buried out there somewhere would be the remains of the old Standard car factory that was in its infancy in Larkin's time. Production finally ceased in 1980, by which time it was owned by British Leyland. There's a still a Standard-Triumph Recreation Club, however, deep in the heart of what's now a business park. These days it hosts the Corner Pocket Jazz and Blues Club. The former jazz correspondent of the Daily Telegraph would have been heartened to know that, I'm sure.

Sure?

Well not quite sure, obviously. Nobody can be sure of anything with regard to Larkin's true feelings on any subject.

Closer to the Suttons' former home were the gardens of houses built in the post-war years. "There's a very large pond beyond that bungalow," Satvinder pointed out.

That mini-lake would have been part of the garden of 127 Beechwood in the days when Larkin was a lad. As for the tennis court that he remembered, it was much closer to the house. "We found it just below the surface when the lawn wasn't growing very well and we had it dug up," I was told by Cathy Wattebot who lives in what is now number 129 , on the other side of the divide, with her husband Derek. Or Professor Derek Holt, to give him his proper title. Both are academics and Cathy stood for the Green Party in the local authority elections of 2018.

"The house was divided into two in 1949," she explained, leading the way from the lawn up some original steep steps, through the conservatory to the imposing former billiard room. Long and well lit, it is now at the heart of the household. No green baize, however. The only thing played there today is the piano.

I have no idea whether Sutton and Larkin were allowed near the billiard table. But I do think it likely that Larkin would have preferred billiards to snooker which, in those days, was considered a game for idlers loafing around in smoky rooms over Burton's the Tailors.

It also seems likely that his journey, on foot or by bike, to or from Beechwood Avenue, would have been broken by a visit to Earlsdon Library. Books were one thing he could never get enough of. Indeed he stole one from those very shelves. As if his father didn't have enough at home!

Typically, Don Lee knew the title. "It was The Senior Commoner by Julian Hall," he'd told me when we'd met in the unlikely setting of Caffe Nero on Piccadilly Station in Don's native Manchester. "It was found in Larkin's collection after his death and given back to the Coventry library service."

Not that, I suspect, too many Coventrians would be clamouring to borrow it. The novel was set in Eton College and, according to a piece that Larkin wrote for The Spectator in 1982, was a huge structure of tiny episodes designed to portray a complex institution at all levels. Apparently he was attracted by its "brittle plangency of style and its studied circumstantial irrelevancy".

Evidently a treasured possession for the light-fingered Philip who would, of course, go on to become an eminent librarian. James Booth, one of the poet's biographers and now an Emeritus Professor at Hull, once told me that he received a stern letter from Larkin in his days as "a Lefty lecturer". Having refused to pay a library fine, Booth was informed that books were stolen more often than we imagined. "Only much later did I read that, in his youth, our eminent librarian had stolen one book from a library in Coventry and another from Blackwells in Oxford."

That "library in Coventry" just happens to be one of my favourite Earlsdon buildings. As a plaque on the solid red-brick frontage reminds us, it was one of three such literary treasures gifted to the city by the Scottish-American philanthropist Andrew Carnegie. In 1912, that was, 10 years before Larkin was born.

It was also two years after the death of Edward VII, yet there's still an Edwardian ornateness about the exterior. The words "PUBLIC LIBRARY" are carved in capitals into an arched and elaborately etched stone inset above the front door. Right at the top are the elephant and castle of Coventry's coat-of-arms, as if to proclaim that this is a municipal building in perpetuity.

If only.

Coventry City Council has largely withdrawn funding from this, the most popular local library in the city, blaming national government for slashing its budget. Now the place is only open three days and two half-days a week.

It wouldn't be open at all were it not for the dedication of volunteers from the local community. As I write, discussions are ongoing over the future of a building that means so much to so many people. Including me. I spent many a Saturday morning in my childhood and adolescence in a similar Carnegie library some 25 miles or so from here.

The ambience then, in the 1950s and '60s, wouldn't have been too different from this place as Larkin would have remembered it in the 1920s and '30s. Same rows of musty hardbacks that nonetheless offered illustrious gateways to different worlds. Same fearsome librarians, proverbially twin-setted, pearled, bulbously bunned or tightly permed, shushing into silence anybody with the effrontery to speak in anything more than a whisper.

Beneath the carved, arched stonework today is a glass door that shoots open as soon as anybody approaches it – on

Mondays, Tuesdays, Thursdays, Friday afternoons and Saturday mornings, anyway. To the left you might hear a group of matrons holding a voluble discussion over coffee and knitting pins. While round to the right, nursery rhymes are occasionally chanted or sung by organised gatherings of infants in the children's section.

There are, needless to say, plenty of new-fangled gadgets that wouldn't have been there in Larkin's day. Or mine. Tables topped by computer screens, for instance, and a digital device for taking out or returning whatever you've borrowed. Easy, once you get the hang of it. You can also take out books on CD or films on DVD for a small charge.

Still available, mind you, are plenty of old-fashioned hardbacks and paperbacks. The poetry section is well stocked. There are four Larkin entries in Penguin's Poems for Life and An Arundel Tomb rounds off the entire book. There could hardly be a more fitting poem for the end of "Life".

Nearby is a copy of Philip Larkin Poems published by Faber and Faber and edited by Martin Amis. Son of Kingsley Amis, of course, and a celebrated novelist in his own right. Despite being "a nine-to-five librarian, who lived for thirty years in a northern city that smelled of fish", Amis junior hails Larkin as "the novelist's poet" and "most definitely this novelist's poet".

Praise indeed, despite the metropolitan Martin's admitted bafflement about his "provinciality" and his behaviour on a personal level on those occasions when they met. After all, his father had known Larkin since their Oxford days. Kingsley apparently read two or three of his poems every night. Yet he returned from friend Philip's funeral in 1985 and sighed, "I sometimes wondered if I ever really knew him".

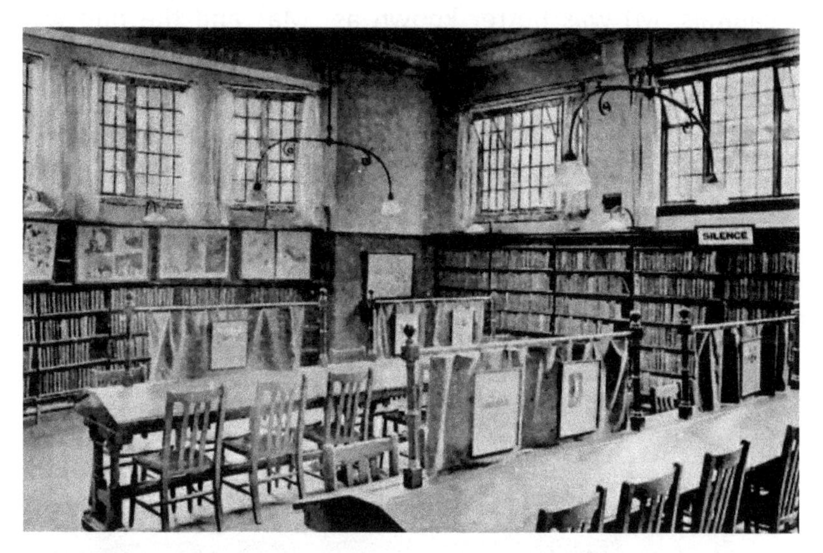

"Shush": Earlsdon Library interior as it would have been when light-fingered Philip stole a book (Earlsdon Research Group)

On my way to borrow this collection, with its illuminating introduction, I noticed a section of the library devoted to Dementia Support – a sympathetic antithesis to Larkin's bleak yet all too haunting poem The Old Fools. Above the shelves were two sepia photographs: one of the library and, nearby, another of the high street that he might have remembered. There are two more photos above the LARGE PRINT section. Thankfully, these books are no longer labelled "FOR THE NEARLY BLIND", as they were in my childhood library in less politically correct days.

As for Larkin's childhood, changes were soon afoot in the City Arms, the pub on the corner diagonally opposite Earlsdon

Library. It's shown in sepia as a small building with a large sign. The name of the landlady, MJ Cooper, is prominently displayed in capitals. MJ was better known as "Ma" and the pub was known as Ma Cooper's long after her death in 1923 and long after the building had been replaced by a much bigger tavern in 1930. Mock-Tudor, if you please, with prints from Shakespeare's plays in almost every room.

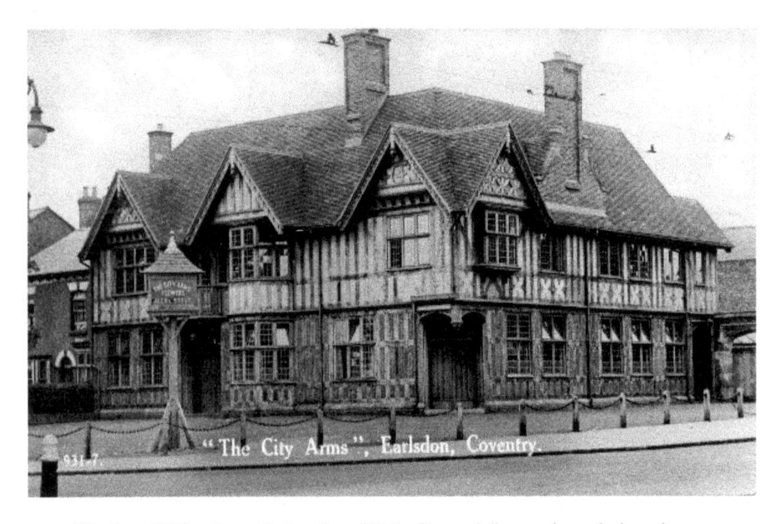

The "new" City Arms that replaced "Ma Cooper's" more homely beer house (Earlsdon Research Group)

Well, the licence in those days was in the hands of the Stratford-based Flowers' brewery. Mary Jane Cooper had been a nanny to the six children of Edgar Flowers until the age of 45 when she'd married a publican, only to be widowed soon afterwards. Compensation came in the form of the keys to the City Arms where she flourished for some 25 years.

She was feared as well as loved, by all accounts. A kindly woman by nature, she stood no nonsense. You didn't mess with

Ma – as troops from the First Battalion of the Royal Munster Fusiliers discovered when they were stationed in Earlsdon in 1915, shortly before being butchered at the Battle of Gallipoli.

By the time the next World War loomed, Larkin may have appeared old enough to get away with savouring a none-too-swift half in the recently expanded and half-timbered City Arms while browsing through a book borrowed (or nicked) from the nearby library. What's more certain is that octogenarian and long-term Earlsdon resident David Wagstaff had paid his first visit – albeit to the pub garden with his grandfather.

"It's one of my earliest memories," he confided. "Granddad used to take me when I was still in a pram. He'd driven a horse and dray for the railways since 1903." That would have been one of the nose-bagged horses that Larkin recalled scattering chaff around the station on his way to and from school (see Chapter Four).

David, a former bio-medical scientist, is an aficionado of a somewhat zippier form of transport. He still drives an open-topped Alvis 1250, built in Coventry in 1928, eight years before he was born over a corner shop in Mayfield Road.

It just so happens that it was in July 1939, that the teenage Larkin was proceeding towards Earlsdon Library or the Suttons' house (or both) when he conceived two particularly vituperate verses called Alvis Victrix, since published by Faber and Faber in their collection of his Early Poems and Juvenilia. The car is described as "a voluptuous monster, painted red, Silently swimming along the Albany Road". But it's those in the car who are the real targets. The passenger is evidently a fellow sixth-former at King Henry's being conveyed to a cricket match with "oiled bat" by his "flabby lecher" of a father. It's the kind of vitriol that would be posted on social media today, if somewhat less poetically.

Albany Road, incidentally, is the main link between Earlsdon, the art-deco Albany Theatre and the Butts Park Arena where Coventry rugby club now play. The road still harbours the splendidly named funeral directors, Grimmett and Timms, founded in 1934. But the Astoria Cinema that Larkin would have remembered has long gone. So, alas, has the second-hand book shop that he wouldn't have remembered but may well have liked.

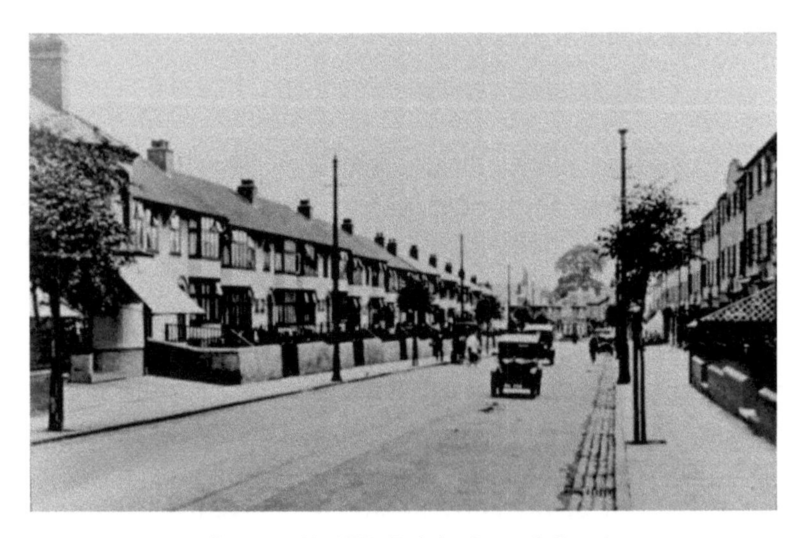

Albany Road in 1927 (Earlsdon Research Group)

I certainly did. It was started by a rum character called Colin Armstrong who moved to Coventry in 1966 to work on the ring road, became involved in the thriving local folk music scene, began collecting books and paintings, dabbled in poetry and has become what you might call an "ale-fellow-well-met" champion of the city's cultural scene. His book shop opened in 1983 and survived for 24 years. Not that it was always open during normal opening hours. Colin liked a pint (still does) and when you saw a sign on the door saying "back in 10 minutes", you knew that he was in the City Arms.

Which is where, come to think of it, we left David Wagstaff. In the garden with his granddad rather a long time ago.

The Earlsdon that he remembered from his childhood was not much different from the one that Larkin would have known. Or indeed the photographer who took those sepia pictures in the library.

At the bottom of the main street, almost opposite the pub, was the Co-operative Society. More recently it has been a shop specialising in the flouncy '50s dresses that the former head librarian at Hull University used to relish, having positioned his chair under the stairs for a surreptitious stare. "The Co-op wanted to expand into the bakery next door but the baker wouldn't have it," David recalled. "Just as well. We kids used to buy lovely large white batches there to eat on our way to school."

Next door was the Empire Butchers, a name that would gladden the heart of Brexiteers were it to make a comeback.

Which seems about as likely as finding New Zealand lamb chops in a Parisian market.

Butchers and bakers were prevalent in pre-war Earlsdon Street. Candlestick-makers? Probably not. But there were iron-mongers where you could buy loose nails in brown paper and much else besides.

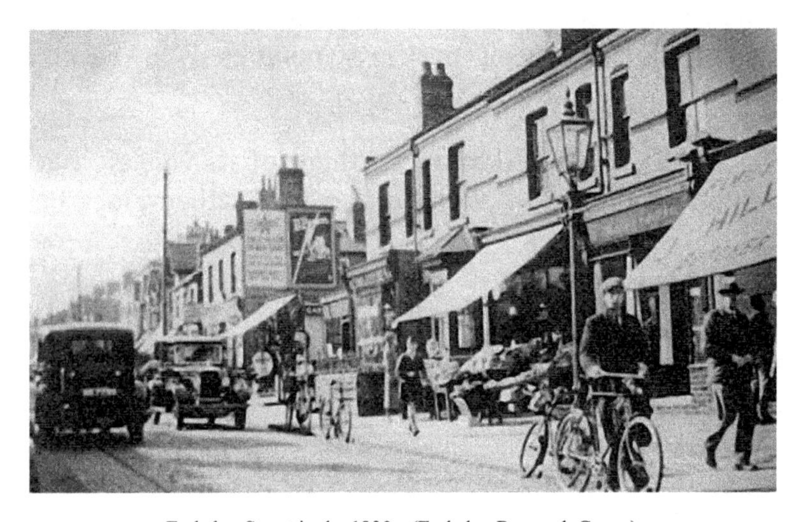

Earlsdon Street in the 1930s (Earlsdon Research Group)

Gents' outfitters rubbed tweedy shoulders with gleaming bike shops. The modern bicycle was not only invented in Coventry but made and sold here in some numbers. Indeed the nail factory on Moor Street, built in 1885 and handsomely restored in recent years as offices and bedsits, had become a cycle manufacturer. It was run by Fred Allard, a top cyclist in the 1890s, who has a road named after him elsewhere in the city.

Earlsdon was full of small-scale manufacturing as well as retailing in Larkin's day, but nail-making didn't last too long once local housewives kicked up a fuss about the effects of soot on their washing. This was not the Black Country, thank you very much. Rather it was one of the more prosperous parts of Coventry. "All brown boots and no breakfast," was how Earlsdoners were dubbed elsewhere in the city – a reference to the prosperity of the watch-makers who could afford a spare pair of boots to go out in. Until, that is, they were largely put out of business by imports from the United States and Switzerland.

Where would they have gone out to, those brown-booted slickers with their leather-strapped and gold-chained tickers?

Possibly Ma Cooper's. Or the Earlsdon Cottage, once a characterful pub in Warwick Street that was still hosting "free and easy" sing-songs and "trad" jazz nights in the late as well as the early 20th century. Or my beloved local, the Royal Oak, still serving the well-kept Bass that the Cottage was once famous for and still standing proudly on the corner of the main street and Moor Street. Or maybe the Albany Social Club, a few doors down, built in 1899 with all sorts of late-Victorian flourishes on the exterior. Some still survive to this day, although the building now has a flat rather than a pitched roof, the top floor having gone missing some time in the post-war years.

Once a month, Jazz Coventry attracts top performers from all over the country to the upstairs function room. Modern jazz, I'm glad to say – the sort of music that Larkin would have found far too funky. He long ago drew the line at Miles Davis and John Coltrane.

Across the tram lines from the Albany in his day stood the Imperial Cinema with its imperiously decorative frontage. "There would be two films Monday to Wednesday," David recalled, "and two different ones from Thursday to Saturday." With the Pathe News in between, needless to say.

As for Larkin's local cinematic memories, they were touched upon in a letter to Jim Sutton in which he recalled the first film that he ever saw. Scarface, apparently, "bringing back Coventry for me . . . and the Rialto and Spon Street and all the pre-bombing features".

Time, perhaps, for a brief break from Earlsdon and a brisk walk to the edge of the city centre where post-war Spon Street is partly lined with mediaeval buildings that survived the Blitz and were relocated there. As a result, it's now a conservation area. The Rialto has long gone. So have the courtyards of terraced housing that once ran off it and provided the customers for the Old Windmill, otherwise known as "Ma Brown's". She was the magisterial matron who held court there between 1940 and 1967, enthroned on a chair adjacent to the piano and the open fire with its inbuilt priest-hole.

Unlike other mediaeval Johnny-come-latelies, the Windmill has stood on the same spot for six centuries. Today there's still an open fireplace as well as three distinctive snugs and an array of well-kept real ales. What's more, you can have anything you like to eat as long as it's a pork pie from the nearby market.

Now let's return, briefly, from Ma Brown's to Ma Cooper's. To the side of the long-since-Wetherspooned City Arms, the long-since-demolished cinema is now a "craft" beer shop. And behind it is a tap room where you can sit on long benches savouring American pale ales or Belgian blonde lagers until well into the evening.

Next door is the Universal Discount Store, a cornucopia of consumer products and hardware. You can buy anything from beach balls to light bulbs, plant food to paint, non-stick saucepans to garden tools, buckets to brackets for your new shelf. And more. Much more. Yes, there are nails and screws on offer. Not loose and wrapped in brown paper, alas. Still, this is as near as you're going to get to a traditional ironmonger in Earlsdon today.

Bakers?

There's a branch of Greggs a few doors from a much-expanded Co-op store and there was, until recently, a "vintage tea-room and delicatessen" specialising in Italian organic loaves.

Butchers?

Just one remains on the main street. A very good one, too. Apart from anything else, he offers at lunchtimes a classic example of the Coventry pièce de résistance: the pork and stuffing batch.

Greengrocers?

A very popular one next door to a longstanding fish and chip shop.

Yet the number of nearby charity shops, to let signs and vans heading up side streets to deliver food ordered on-line is a sign of the times. So is the long locked-and-barred frontage of Pennycook's, jewellers and watch menders. Ray Pennycook was born a few months after Philip Larkin but lived to be 95. To see him squinting through an eyeglass at the interior of your wristwatch was a like a glimpse into Earlsdon's past. At least his long-time assistant Helen Cunningham still sells jewellery, albeit at the back of an antique shop offering items that seemed commonplace in my childhood, let alone Pennycook's and Larkin's.

Earlsdon has its fair share of cafe-bars and coffee-bars, as well as restaurants – Indian and Italian, Turkish and Thai. Not to mention a Polynesian cocktail bar.

Somehow I suspect that Larkin might have preferred a pint or a couple of large gins in the bar of the nearby Criterion Theatre. In his day, mind you, this building in Berkley Road South housed a Methodist Sunday School rather than a playhouse for thespians. Amateur thespians, I should add, although "amateurish" is not a word that comes to mind when I'm sitting in the second row marvelling at the performance of someone I last saw having a coffee in Millsy's cafe-bar or a pint in the Oak.

Somebodies, like nobodies, pop up anywhere.

During the Earlsdon May Day Festival of 2018, the Criterion staged a stunning performance of a short musical called Larkin about Jazz, first in the theatre car park and then in the main street. As this book goes to press, an extended version is set to be performed at the theatre as Jazz Coventry's November gig.

A heartening sign, perhaps, that it's not just staff from Philip's former school who are prepared to recognise and even celebrate a great poet who was born and spent his formative years in the next City of Culture.

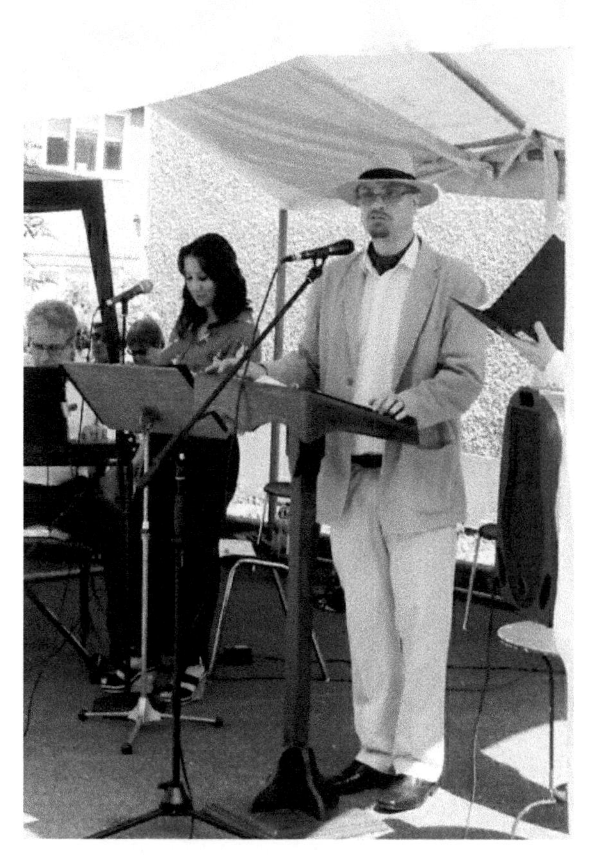

Nicol Cortese and Hugh Sorrill of the Citerion Theatre recreating Larkin's love of jazz at the Earlsdon Festival

(Earlsdon Echo)

CHAPTER 7

Took Photos of the Rebuilding

"Some bits are awful; others are not bad," he wrote to Monica Jones before going on to describe it as "clumsy and rather graceless . . . lacking intelligence at all levels, but not without a certain needless opulence in parts."

I'm sure I don't have to tell you who "he" is. Yes, the "hard-to-please librarian", as the eminent historian David Kynaston describes Larkin in his tome Modernity Britain 1957-62 (Bloomsbury) from which that opening quote is taken.

As it happens, the poet was referring to the "new" university library in Hull. But it could just as easily have been the "new" city centre that had risen out of the rubble of immediate post-war Coventry.

For one whose childhood had apparently been "unspent" there, he came back more often than you might imagine. Even took photographs of the rebuilding process – "quite stunning" ones according to Philip Pullen. (None of them appear in Richard Bradford's book on Larkin's photography, however.)

Did he like what he had focused his lens on?

Probably not.

Comments from him about Europe's first pedestrian precinct being built in the city of the motor car are difficult to come by. Still, I suspect that Pullen was spot on when he told me, "I don't think he'd have been enamoured."

For one thing, Larkin was naturally a traditionalist rather than a modernist. For another, his family home was destined to be buried under a ring road that was to be a vital part in avoiding traffic congestion in the heart of the new city. For yet another, he was more upset than he would have cared to admit by the sheer scale of the destruction wreaked by the Luftwaffe on the place where he had grown up.

"The devastation continued to haunt him for years," Andrew Motion pointed out in his 1994 biography Philip Larkin: A Writer's Life (Faber and Faber). Among the evidence quoted to confirm that point were extracts from Jill, the first of two novels written by one who would later make his name through a more concise literary form. Jill was written when the poet was 21, just three years after he had left Coventry for Oxford.

The main character, John Kemp, makes the return journey towards the end of the book. Except that Coventry has become Huddlesford, which sounds more northern – a conflation of Huddersfield and Bradford, just as JB Priestley had done in 1929 with his Bruddersfield in The Good Companions.

No matter. Larkin was obviously drawing on personal experience when he described Kemp witnessing the first bombed house that he had ever seen. There were "broken bricks, lurching floors and laths sticking out like delicate broken bones".

More details are forthcoming of what it was like to wander through destroyed streets that had been all too familiar. There are also passages that allow Larkin to express sensitivities that he would have been reluctant to admit in any public pronouncements.

As he picks his way towards the family home, "noticing half-bricks driven by fierce explosions into the hedges", Kemp sees everything that irritated him about his parents transformed into loveable qualities. He would do anything, renounce everything that he had ever said about them, if only he could find that they were still alive.

Kemp does. Larkin did. Cue palpable relief all round. They may "fuck you up" but, hey, they're still your Mum and Dad.

Larkin apparently blamed his father for dragging the family to Germany in the 1930s and giving him a "hatred of abroad". Yet on the next page of A Writer's Life he is quoted as describing his school trip to Brussels, Antwerp and the Ardennes as "the best and jolliest holiday" he had ever spent.

Contradictory?

No change there.

Motion's biography didn't do a lot for Larkin's reputation among what the late, great political columnist Alan Watkins used to call "the chattering classes". How could someone capable of expressing such sensitivity and subtlety on the page be such a racist, misogynist and "porn addict" in real life?

Maybe that helps to explain why he wasn't admitted to Poets' Corner until 2016, over 30 years after his death. Then again, if morality was a necessary qualification, the Corner would be confined to the smallest adjoining walls of a broom cupboard in Westminster Abbey.

The Coventry that young Philip and his fellow sixth-formers at Henry VIII returned to after their jolly-boys trip to Belgium was about to "change, change utterly". Whether, to continue quoting Yeats rather than Larkin, a "terrible beauty was born" from the resurrection of the central core remains a matter of debate to this day.

Unlike Dresden, one of its many twin cities, Coventry did not set about rebuilding its past. The City Council had already begun knocking down mediaeval streets before a single German bomb had been dropped.

Coventrians, along with any number of incomers from elsewhere, didn't just build motor cars; they also bought them in significant numbers. Pay was higher than in most provincial cities and it seems likely that factories gave a decent discount to employees wanting to purchase the products of their labours.

Broadgate was at the heart of the city then and now – "then" being nigh-on 80 years ago. In 1939 it was a wide street that just happened to be at the point where the main route to Birmingham intersected with the main route to Leicester. On Saturday afternoons, when Larkin and Jim Sutton would be rooting through jazz records in nearby Hertford Street, the place would be rammed with trams and buses, bikes and cars.

"There was incredible congestion," Peter Walters told me as we strolled across what has long been a square for pedestrians only. "The Council had already built Trinity Street and Corporation Street to divert some of the traffic [demolishing mediaeval backwaters such as Little Butcher Row and Palmer Lane in the process]. Now they were desperate to reduce traffic in Broadgate."

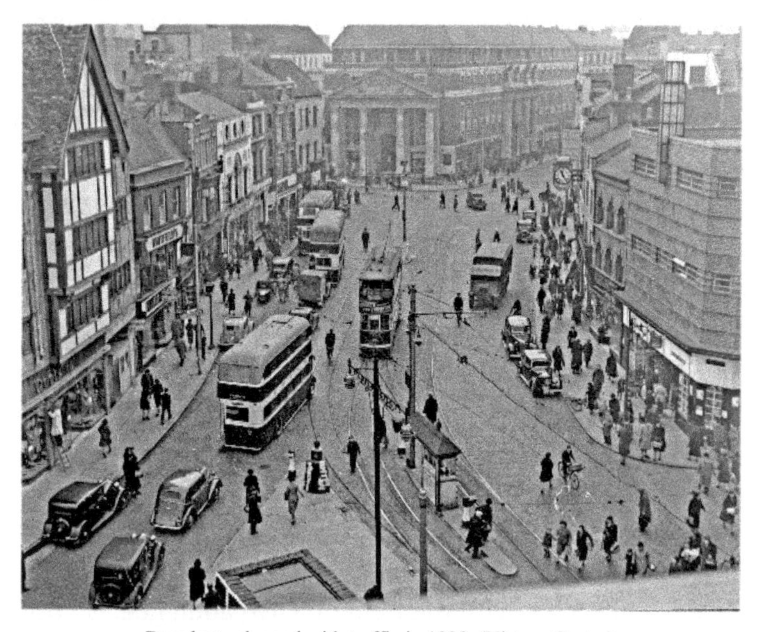

Broadgate clogged with traffic in 1939 (History Centre)

Sydney Larkin had already been told by councillors that he would have to find money in his budget to pay for the services of a city architect. Donald Gibson had taken up his post in 1938, aged 29, and was already impatient to clear away impediments to his modernist vision. Before the first German bomb had landed, indeed, plans were being drawn up to demolish more of the sort of streets that would later become architectural treasures in places such as York and Chester.

Young Philip would have taken those ancient, narrow nooks for granted in his youth as he headed for the central library. On page 28 of A Writer's Life, Motion quotes him reminiscing fondly about that building "nestling at the foot of the un-bombed cathedral, filled with tall, antiquated bookcases . . . with my ex-schoolfellow Ginger Thompson at the counter to stamp the books you chose and the Golden Cross nearby".

Part of the library survived the war. Indeed it was still there when I came to Coventry in 1981. Not for long, however. In 1986 it relocated, lock, stock and barrels of books, to the more expansive spaces of the former Locarno dance hall in Smithford Way, part of the post-war precinct.

Larkin had died the previous year. He would never return to see the library that had helped to feed his fevered imagination re-established in the glass-fronted building where The Specials had made a triumphant return to their home city after a lengthy American tour and, a few years previously, Chuck Berry had recorded a hit single with the help of a live audience. No doubt the poet and librarian would have been hugely impressed by the imagery, density and complexity of My Ding-a-ling.

Time, perhaps, to return briefly to Broadgate in 1939. There were shops along both sides, broken up by the imposing portals of the National Westminster Bank, which survived the blitz, and the King's Head Hotel which did not.

"It was Victorian and not of huge interest architecturally," said Walters, a walking authority on Coventry. "But it was the place where businessmen mingled with big-wigs from the

Council, and I suspect that Sydney Larkin would have gone for the odd snifter."

The City Treasurer had been in Broadgate (shopping rather than supping a snifter) on the lunchtime of August 25 when a bomb exploded in the basket left outside Astley's the jewellers at 1.32pm precisely. It missed him "by a whisker", according to Philip Pullen.

Elsie Ansell was not so lucky. She was a 21-year-old shop assistant who was about to be married and was gazing into Astley's front window when the bomb went off. Her remains were later buried in the church where her wedding had been booked.

Another four people were killed and some 70 more suffered non-fatal injuries. Two members of the Irish Republican Army, Peter Barnes and James McCormick, were subsequently hanged at Winson Green Prison in Birmingham.

The Midland Daily Telegraph had reported that the IRA's bomb had left Broadgate resembling "a miniature battlefield". Understandable at the time, no doubt, but all too soon that battlefield would be put in perspective.

Within a couple of days of November 14, 1940, Gibson and the City Council leader George Hodgkinson had plans for the radical rebuilding of Coventry's city centre spread out on the floor of an office in the Council House, a blessed blitz survivor.

It would be too cynical to suggest that they were pleased that the Luftwaffe had saved them the trouble of demolishing the mediaeval core of the city. They must have been as shaken as anyone else by the carnage of "that night". Hodgkinson's nine-year-old son had been sheltering under the stairs of the family home in Coundon while he and his wife were busy trying to put out incendiary bombs and the roof almost caved in. As he bent over Gibson's futuristic plans, I suspect that there would also be an element of "who do you think you are kidding, Mr Hitler, if you think this city's done"?

Sydney Larkin may have felt slightly differently, having kept his notorious model of the aforesaid Fuhrer on his office mantelpiece until shortly before the outbreak of war. As City Treasurer, he may also have felt a little queasy about the sheer cost of the rebuilding process.

If so, he needn't have bothered too much.

In 1941, soon after residents had endured another four nights of bombing, a civic deputation was summoned to lunch in London. Claridge's was the venue, Sir John (later Lord) Reith the host. Yes, that Reith – the one who'd founded the BBC.

In his war-time capacity as First Commissioner of Works, he urged his Midland visitors to plan a bold and comprehensive resurrection and not worry too much about the money. "Coventry would be a test case," he assured them, "not for me and my authority, but for the Government and for England."

If Sydney was relieved by that Reithian proclamation committing national government to shoulder its share of the expenditure, he wasn't entirely impressed by Gibson's plans. He gave a speech to the Coventry Rotary Club in 1947 calling for more shops and fewer flower-beds in Broadgate.

As for Philip, he kept a copy of the Coventry Evening Telegraph's coverage of that speech. Sent to him by his mother, no doubt. Eva continued to take the "Cov Tel" long after she'd left Coventry.

But whatever the Larkins, senior and junior, thought of the rebuilding process, the Precinct has had its fair share of admirers. In the 1960s, the eminent architecture critic Ian Nairn described it as "probably the best thing of its kind in Europe". He felt that "the spaces are all right, and the basic feel of the place is all right".

"All right" sounds a bit like damning with faint praise, but Nairn could be outspoken in his criticism of post-war modernism. Particularly if he felt that it was being obscured by commercial intruders. He died in 1983, shortly before that process in Coventry began in earnest.

Gibson's Precinct was not a "concrete jungle". It was built largely in mellow red brick. Westmorland slate was used for the pillars holding up shop canopies and the underside of those canopies was lined with dark wood. Still is in parts. And the slate pillars and facings are still there, albeit sometimes smudged and cracked with age and lack of maintenance.

As for the commercial intrusions, they began in earnest with the growing dependence on a retail economy in the 1980s. Never mind red brick and Westmoreland slate, and never mind pleas from the Twentieth Century Society about the despoiling of Coventry's post-war legacy. One side of Smithford Way was demolished to make way for the back end of the West Orchards

Shopping Centre, light grey in colour and resembling a giant convector heater.

Later an escalator was installed to convey shoppers from the Upper Precinct to the upper reaches of West Orchards. Apparently I described it as resembling a derailed train in an article written for The Independent in 1991 – "accurately" so, according to a recent Nooks and Corners column in Private Eye.

Well, at least the latest redevelopment includes plans to demolish the escalator along with some depressingly grey concrete intruders from the 1960s and '70s. Other obstructions to views of Broadgate are also to "bite the bulldozer".

At time of writing, however, there are still ongoing conflicts not only with the Twentieth Century Society but also Historic England. Private developers' plans for more glitzy shop frontages do not fit well with the conservationists' view of a city centre that is now a Heritage Action Zone. As the Private Eye column pointed out, "Historic England jointly signed the HAZ agreement that helped Coventry become the City of Culture in 2021". There were hints at the time that Gibson's precinct may be registered as a conservation area – "a rare honour for post-war architecture".

Be that as it may, one commercial intruder that won't be going any time soon is the Cathedral Lanes Shopping Centre. Built with Kuwaiti money and opened in 1990, it succeeded in obscuring part of the old cathedral spire that Gibson was keen to keep in full view from the Upper Precinct.

What the shopping centre didn't succeed in doing was to attract many shops. And most of those it did attract closed down not too long after opening. Only one survived for any length of time, which means that a branch of Wilko now backs on to the site that once harboured Larkin's beloved library.

At least the part of Cathedral Lanes that fronts on to Broadgate has been taken up by restaurants. Diners sitting outside Wagamama's, Las Iguana's or the Cosy Club have two potential views of Godiva. One is the rear end of herself and her horse, as portrayed in William Reid Dick's elegant 1949 bronze.

The other view of Godiva comes every hour on the hour. Whether the clock named after her strikes one or two pm, eleven am or twelve noon, out she comes. Out too comes the hideous head of Peeping Tom, leering down on her before she disappears again through another door on the far side of the balcony. It's splendidly tacky and makes me smile if ever I happen to be passing when she makes her appearance.

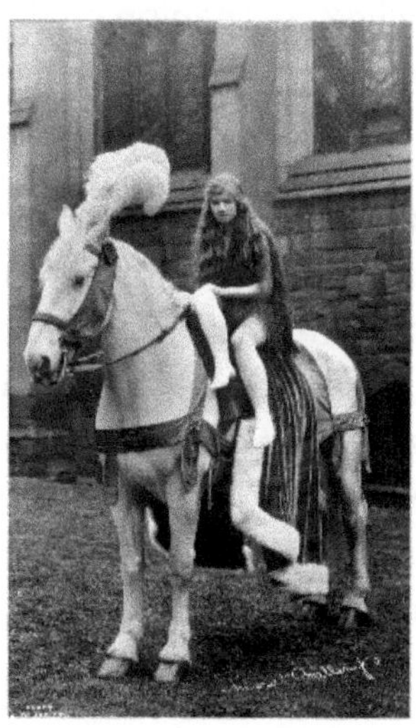

Miss Muriel Mellerup ready to giddy-up as Lady Godiva in 1929
(History Centre)

As for Larkin, he was a bit of a Peeping Tom himself. As mentioned in earlier chapters, at the university library in Hull he positioned his chair under the stairs for surreptitious stares up skirts as they flared. And in more youthful days, he used to join his father on his office balcony at Coventry Council House to gaze down on whichever local beauty had been chosen to don the wig and body-stocking to lead the annual Godiva Festival.

Gibson, or Sir Donald as he would later become, left Coventry for Nottinghamshire in 1955 – coincidentally the same year that Larkin briefly viewed his home city from a train window and was inspired to write I Remember, I Remember.

Had it been after April rather than "early in the cold New Year", he and his travelling companion could have broken their lengthy journey, trudged or taxied into town and put up at the Leofric.

Would have cost them a bit, mind you – 37 shillings (£1.85) for a single room with breakfast. Quite steep for the times. But then this was the first hotel built in a British city with British money since the war and no expense had been spared. Never mind the blitzed King's Head; this place was the last word in luxury. Seventy five of the 108 bedrooms were en-suite. With connections for electric razors, indeed, as well as rails for the ladies to dry their nylons.

At the end of the Leofric's first year in business, manager John Wearmouth revealed that there had been some 3,460 foreign visitors. Nearly half were American.

The Warwickshire gin-and-Jag set had swanned into the place as well. Bar takings were "colossal", according to Wearmouth, helped perhaps by the charismatic cocktail barman Ray Rastall who was there from the opening until 1986 when he moved to reopen Ray's Bar in the nearby High Street.

It helped that that not far away was the Coventry Theatre – or the Hippodrome as it would have been known in Larkin's youth. It had opened in 1937 in classic Art Deco style and somehow the Luftwaffe had missed it. Philip was taken by his parents to see dance bands led by the likes of Billy Cotton and Harry Roy shortly before he developed a taste for more sophisticated music from the deep south of America rather than the south-east of England.

Among the early guests at the Leofric were Beryl Reid, Tommy Cooper and Gracie Fields for whom the irrepressible Ray conjured up an "Our Gracie" cocktail.

The stars kept coming. Among them were Harry Secombe and Tommy Steele. Later the Stones rolled in and a suite was provided for Dolly Parton.

Such glamour, such glitz, such prominent . . .

It couldn't last.

And it didn't. By 1985 the theatre variously known as the Hippodrome, the Coventry and, more recently, the Apollo had become the Gala Bingo Hall. The Leofric had lost its allure. But it limped on into the 21st century until, in 2008, it was transformed into a Travelodge budget hotel.

Not for long, however. The building that once housed Ray's Bar, a ballroom and the Silver Grill Restaurant is now given over to student apartments.

Coventry University has taken over large parts of the city centre, and good luck to it. It was recently given a gold rating for teaching, putting it ahead of any other former polytechnic and indeed quite a few long-established Russell Group universities. Along with Warwick University, it's helping to transform the place once written off as a ghost town into a city of dreaming aspirers.

The former Odeon Cinema on Jordan Well is now used by the Faculty of Arts and Humanities and named after Ellen Terry, the fabled star of the stage in Victorian times. She was born in the city in 1847 but, as part of a theatrical family, she was soon on the road. Unlike Larkin, she would have left the city long before she was 18. Yet she is remembered not only with her own building but also a blue plaque high on a side-wall at the junction of Broadgate and the Upper Precinct.

The wall borders a branch of Top Shop that in Larkin's day would have been the site of the city's market hall. No, it didn't survive the bombing. Yes, it did make a comeback – eventually – reopening in 1958 a site some few hundred yards away.

In the egalitarian spirit of the post-war world, it was circular to ensure that no one stallholder had an advantage over another. In fact, it was the antithesis of the Leofric, attracting what Larkin would dismissively have referred to as a "cut-price crowd". (Admittedly he used that expression about shoppers in Hull, but then he also referred to Hull as "Coventry-on-sea".)

Sixty years on and some things haven't changed at the market. There are still stalls a-plenty offering an abundance of fresh fruit and veg that's not packed in plastic. Another offers such delicacies as tripe, black pudding and chitterlings. Yum-yum. Many of the cut-price crowd in the poet's Coventry days would have been licking their lips at the prospect of dining on a pig's stomach, congealed blood and/or small intestines.

Some things have changed, however. There are fewer fish stalls and between two of the survivors is a butcher selling halal meat. At the centre of the market, meanwhile, venerable Sikhs chew the fat through abundant beards close to the longstanding children's roundabout that seems a suitable central core for a circular building.

The circularity can sometimes make it difficult to re-discover the entrance that you came in by. There are several exits that can deposit you in different parts of the city. But the most prominent entrance and exit is just off the Lower Precinct, still hailed by the conservationists as a classic example of Festival of Britain architecture. Despite, that is, some much-disputed modern intrusions, including a glass roof.

Plans by the City Council to demolish the circular former burger bar at the LP's hub were staunchly opposed by English Heritage in the early '90s. "Save this?" screamed a headline in the Evening Telegraph. "They must be joking!" But save it they did. A building that always looked as though it was designed to revolve festively if set to music is now a thriving branch of Caffè Nero.

Some 50 yards away, at one end of the Lower Precinct, is an equally thriving branch of Waterstones and at the other is the relocated Cullen Mural. It's a strikingly colourful ceramic by the influential architect and urban designer Gordon Cullen, commissioned in 1957 by the City Planning and Redevelopment Committee to illustrate and celebrate the city's post-war rebirth.

There are all sorts of images in there, from watch-makers to car manufacturers, the Leofric to the Belgrade. And one small section is devoted to a building still under construction at the time. Many years later, it was described as "a magnificent, optimistic and bold response to the horrors of war".

That's not a quote from Larkin, needless to say. It came from the BBC's arts editor Will Gompertz who was asked by Historic England to select his top 10 for their project Irreplaceable: A History of England in 100 Places.

Two cathedrals were included in Gompertz's chart-toppers. One was St Paul's and I'm sure I don't have to spell out the name of the other.

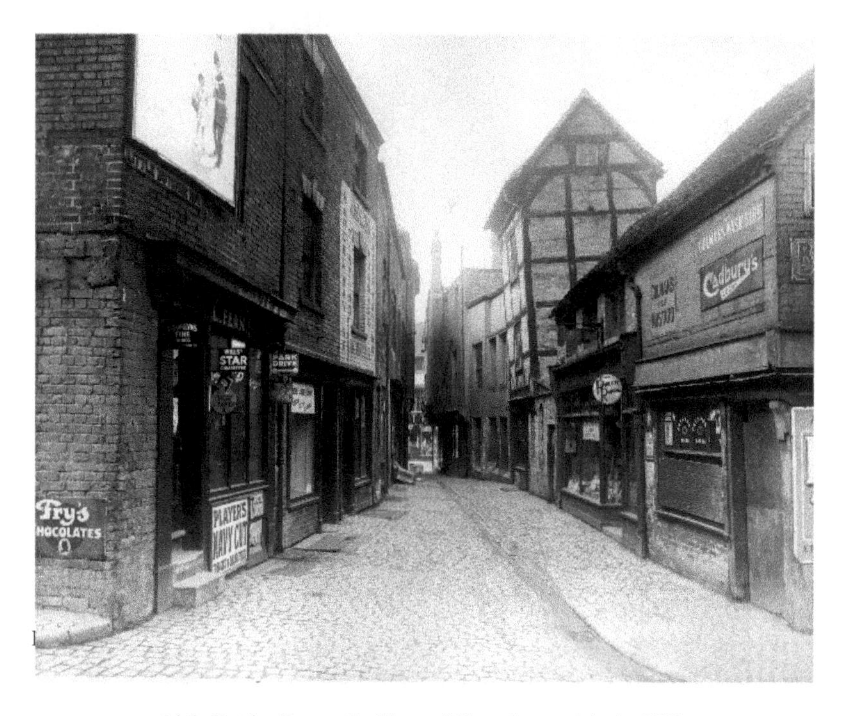

Little Butcher Row as Larkin would have known it in the 1930s
(History Centre)

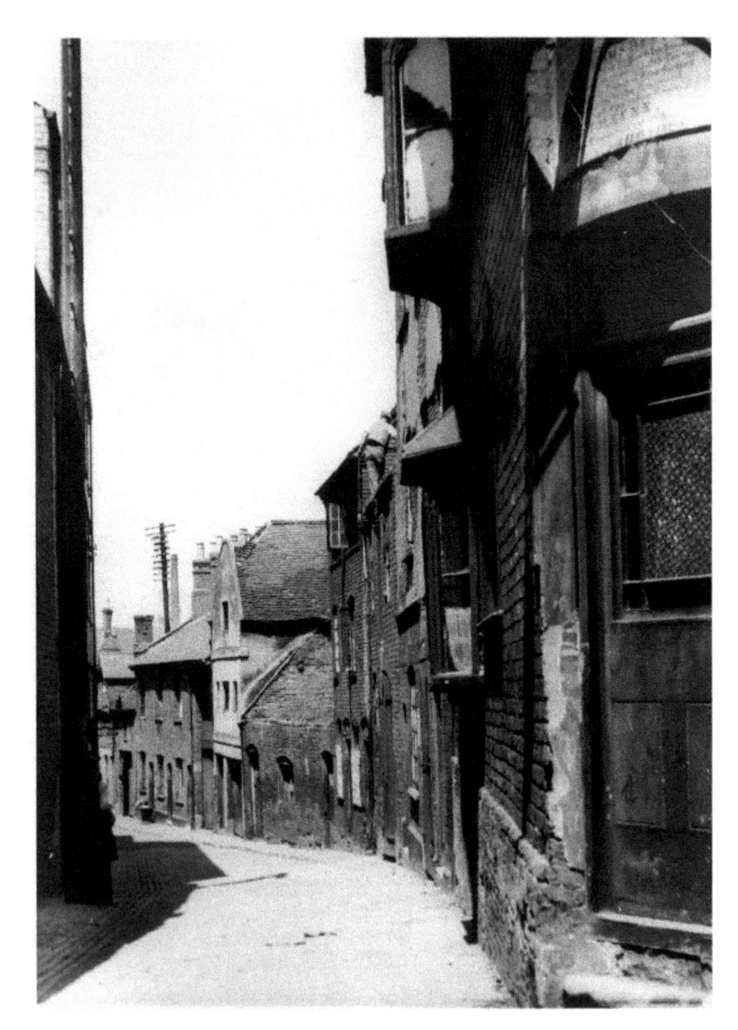

Palmer Lane as Larkin would have known it in the 1930s
(History Centre)

CHAPTER 8

Honoured in the Cathedral, Danced to the Beatles

The consecration came about in 1962, between Ipswich winning the Football League and the Beatles' Love Me Do. An Annus Mirabilis it was not, however, unless you happened to be Alf Ramsey or Ringo Starr.

By October that year the Cuban Missile Crisis had made the threat of nuclear extinction a distinct possibility. Which seemed particularly cruel only a few months after the architectural gem at the heart of "the city of peace and reconciliation" had embodied the hope of a better world born out of resurrection from widespread destruction.

The great and the good were there for the unveiling of Coventry's new cathedral on May 25, including the Queen, Princess Margaret and the Archbishop of Canterbury, Michael Ramsey. Benjamin Britten had had his War Requiem premiered for the occasion, and some of the major artists of the day could cast an appreciative eye over their works, framed as they were by the inspirational setting created by Sir Basil Spence.

Philip Larkin was not there. But he did visit the cathedral on at least two occasions. One was to see his niece Rosemary receiving her degree from Warwick University. The other was to be honoured by Warwick himself in 1973 – with a D.Lit, otherwise known as a Doctorate of Letters. Somehow it seemed appropriate for one who used the postal service with almost as much regularity as many "Tweeters" prod their phones today.

In a letter to Maeve Brennan written straight after the ceremony, he described spotting his mother's former maid, Betty, and her husband looking on in their best clothes. "Very touching," he commented.

What he didn't appear to be touched by was Spence's visionary feat of linking the ruins of the old cathedral with the new. All he had to say on the subject was that the lengthy procession of those being honoured "went all round" what remained of the building where he had been christened in 1922 and then down the steps to "the new one".

He made no comment on Sir Jacob Epstein's stunning statue of St Michael's victory over the Devil; or Graham Sutherland's neck-stretching tapestry soaring above the high altar; or Elisabeth Frink's carved eagle lectern; or, indeed, on John Piper's extraordinary windows.

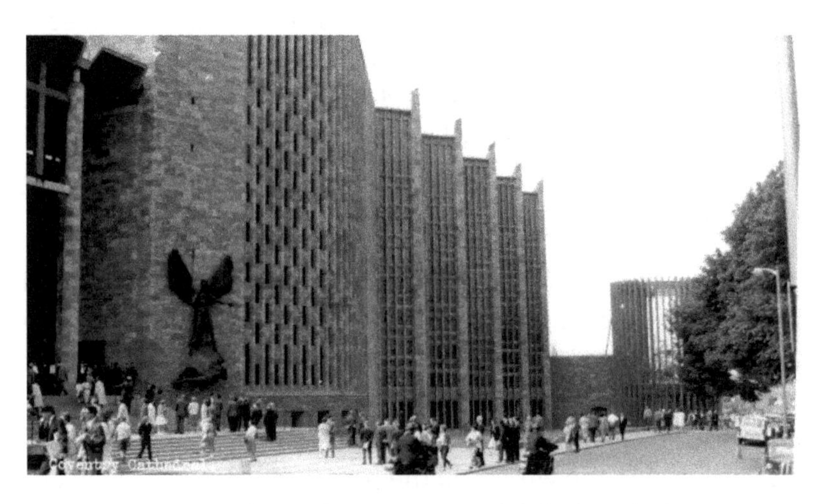

The exterior of Sir Basil Spence's "new" cathedral as it was in 1960
(History Centre)

The Baptistry Window is, to me, the jewel in the crown. On a dull day it cheers you up. On a bright day it dazzles. There are no haloes, no blessed virgins, no crucifixion; just an overwhelming sense of abstract vibrancy. Asked if it symbolised anything, the artist responded, "No, not really – other than a burst of glory."

As a designated war artist, Piper had somehow driven himself to Coventry from Oxford on November 15, 1940, two days before Larkin made it back. Piper headed for what was left of the old cathedral and found what he called "a grey, meal-coloured stack in the foggy close, redder as one came nearer, and still hot and wet from fire and water, finally presenting itself as a series of gaunt red-grey facades stretching eastwards from the dusty but erect tower and spire".

He started work on his vivid picture of those ruins there and then. Rather than be seen sketching amid so much chaos and devastation, death and injury, he talked his way into a nearby solicitor's office where a secretary solicitously offered him her seat with a prime view from the window.

Seventy eight years on, that memorable image was one of many of his glowingly distinctive works displayed at an exhibition of Piper's legacy at the Mead Gallery, part of Warwick Arts Centre (which, as you may have gathered by now, is part of Coventry). The picture was on loan, as it happened, from the Herbert Museum and Art Gallery, next door to Coventry University.

We shall be returning to the Herbert shortly. But first let's take in the view from the entrance to the gallery's impressive

2008 extension that seems to blend in seamlessly with the cathedral across University Square.

Every time I look at the modernist masterpiece from here I feel thankful that, in 1951, the Reconstruction Committee chose Spence's visionary design ahead of 218 others laid out before them.

Sir Giles Gilbert Scott's plans had been rejected in 1942, while war was still raging. Scott had redesigned the House of Commons in Gothic form and his plans for Coventry Cathedral would have been similarly traditional.

That may well have appealed more to Larkin. When it came to religion, he all too typically described himself as not just an agnostic but an "Anglican agnostic".

And Spence?

"He saw an ark of British arts and crafts, a treasure chest holding the best and most beautiful things of the age, sending into the future the work of hands that had known war and were now building for justice and for peace."

That's a direct quote from Sarah Moss's novel The Tidal Zone (Granta, 2016). The main character is a stay-at-home dad who happens to be researching an academic thesis on Spence and the cathedral in those rare moments when he's not obsessing about the health of his daughters.

As for the author, she's Associate Professor of Creative Writing at Warwick University and, yes, this is a work of fiction. But it also offers a fascinating insight into the real life of Spence and how he, "who had first seen the stripped bones of churches in French villages in the war, still saw sunlight transmitted by bright glass". . .

It's all too easy to forget what the resurrection of Coventry Cathedral meant to so many of the generation who had been through the war. As one born four years after it ended, I was brought up on war-time stories, many of them from my mother.

She had been living in central London when the bombs started falling and spent night after night in the deep-level air-raid shelters at one or another of the underground stations. It was crowded, to say the least. The stench of all those bodies crammed together, some resolutely cheerful, most brave-faced but fearful, was something she never forgot.

Early one Saturday evening in 1966, by which time she had long been a resident of Birmingham, she returned from a visit to the new cathedral some 20 miles or so down the road and couldn't stop talking about it. Her eyes were agleam with excitement, as though she couldn't quite believe what she had just witnessed.

I was 17 at the time and getting ready to go out on the town and "on the pull". Dancehalls full of girls were my preoccupation rather than a cathedral full of art-works.

But something must have lodged in my sub-consciousness. I remembered Mum's words and her overwhelming sense of joy when I first clapped eyes on Coventry Cathedral the following year in the heady days of the so-called "summer of love".

Sexual intercourse had been invented four years earlier, according to Larkin. Rather late for him, although he could read the paperback version of Lady Chatterley's Lover while listening to the Beatles first LP.

Larkin? The Beatles?

Not as far-fetched as it sounds. Yes, he no doubt had something droll to say in 1968 when John Lennon and Yoko Ono arrived in Coventry in a white Rolls Royce to plant two acorns in the cathedral grounds and encircled them with a white bench. Peace and love and all that, even if the acorns were soon dug up and the plaque attached to the bench was also stolen by fans. As for the bench, that was moved by the cathedral authorities, much to the displeasure of Lennon who sent his driver to pick it up and bring it home.

Larkin's muse Maeve Brennan was a bit of a Beatles fan herself, according to Don Lee who interviewed her at her home in Cottingham, Hull, shortly before her death in 2003. "She showed me a copy of one of her albums and one track had been played so often that it was almost worn away," he recalled.

I'm Happy Just to Dance With You was the track, A Hard Day's Night the album. And who had Maeve been happy to dance with?

The jazz critic of the Daily Telegraph, no less. He may have been happy just to dance with Maeve, but I suspect that he may well have drawn the curtains first. He wouldn't have wanted any passers-by glimpsing a bald and bespectacled, outwardly respectable poet shuffling about to pop music after a hard day at the library.

Now try to put behind you, if you can, that image of Maeve and Phil grooving around behind drawn curtains. It's time to return from Cottingham to Coventry Cathedral where there has recently been some good news.

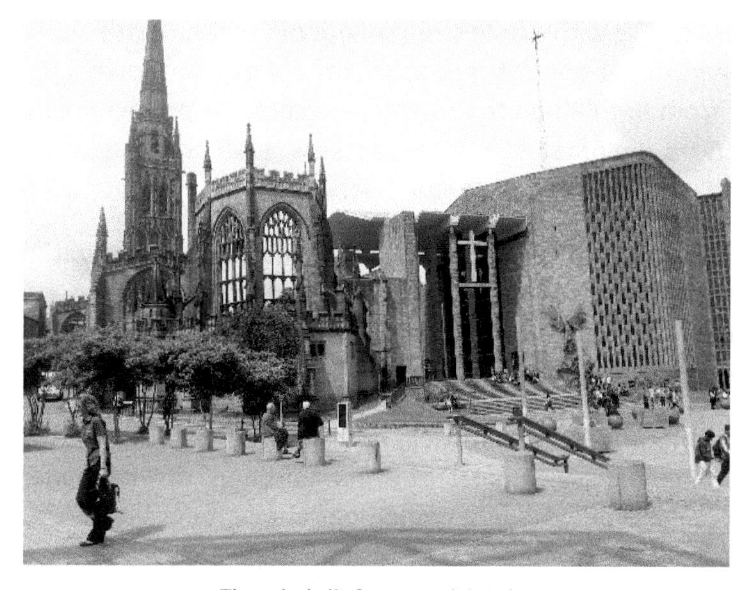

The cathedral's frontage as it is today

Admission charges for visitors have been abolished. At one time they'd risen to eight quid – a little off-putting, even for devotees like me. Although I share Larkin's agnosticism, I also share the view of the BBC's Will Gompertz about the building's boldness and magnificence and greatly admire Spence's determination to make his vision a reality in a cash-strapped post-war world.

The acoustics are not perfect, I'm told by people who know about these things, but visually there's much to admire and inspire. And one of the most inspirational elements is the goodwill bestowed upon it from so many donors from so many lands beyond these shores.

Dwarfed by the "glory" of Piper's Baptistry Window is a huge boulder with a hole scooped out of the top. That's the font. It weighs in at about three tons. Yet it was transported all the way from Bethlehem to Coventry – a complex project involving a retired diplomat as well as packers, craters and steamship brokers, all of whom gave their services free.

New Zealand-born artist John Hutton came up with the vast glass wall of the West Screen that frames the ruins, enhancing the sense that the old and new cathedrals are inextricably linked.

The magnificent mosaic floor in the Chapel of Unity not only encompasses images of every continent on the planet; it also makes you wish you could float above it in case you leave a mark on such a vibrant work of art. Designed by Swedish artist Einar Forseth, apparently, and a gift from the people of Sweden.

As for chapel windows – yet more dazzling stained glass – they're by the artist Margaret Trahearne, born in Westcliff-on-Sea. Another gift from abroad, mind you: this time from the German churches.

I could go on and on. And on. But perhaps it's time to move on, across the University Square towards the Herbert, another treasure-chest of art at the heart of the next City of Culture.

On the way it's worth a glance back. Back up the cobbled part of Bayley Lane on the other side of the ruins, past Drapers'

Hall and St Mary's Hall to the half-timbered buildings just beyond. Back in time to the Coventry that Larkin remembered with some affection. The library was just beyond. So was the Golden Cross. Still is.

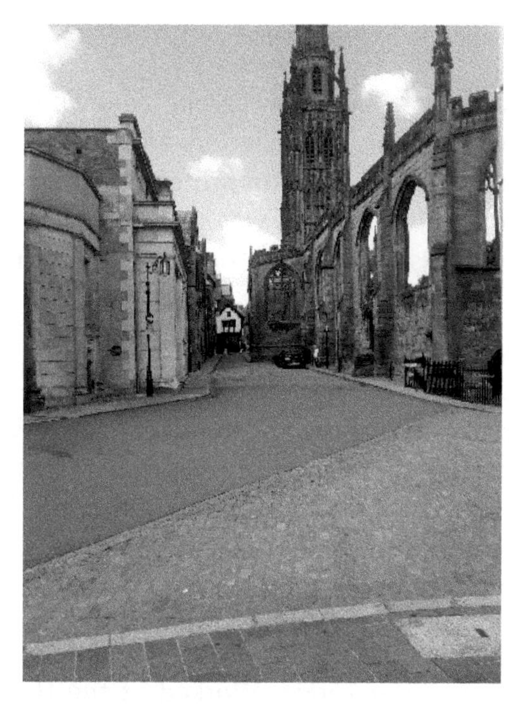

Bayley Lane as it is today with Draper's Hall on the left, St Mary's Hall beyond and the cathedral ruins opposite.

St Michael's Cathedral still stretches along one side of the street. Admittedly there would have been a roof upon it and more than the odd fragment of glass in the window frames when he was christened there, exactly forty years before "the new one" opened its doors to visitors from near and far.

Indeed it would soon become "the premier place of pilgrimage for an anxious, searching and hoping generation", according to John Hewitt who was curator of the nearby Herbert from 1957 to '72.

Hewitt was a poet who, like Larkin "enjoyed that rare combination of popular appreciation and critical acclaim", according to Adrian Smith, emeritus professor of modern history at Southampton University. He was also "unashamedly non-metropolitan" and disliked pop art "or indeed any other fashion of the day".

Remind you of anyone?

"It's hard to envisage the two men agreeing on very much else, other than the importance of [WH] Auden in influencing their early work," says Professor Smith, author of The City of Coventry: A Twentieth Century Icon (IB Taurus, 2005), from which that quote and the ones in the paragraph above are taken.

The professor was born in the city. Went to Henry VIII School, albeit long after Larkin. Worked at the Herbert as a museum assistant just before leaving for university in 1970 and indeed during subsequent vacations. Hewitt had seemed a somewhat remote figure and the young Smith was in awe of him, although he had "no idea that he was one of Ireland's premier poets".

He had been deputy director of the Belfast Museum and Art Gallery in the early 1950s when Larkin was sub-librarian at Queen's University. Hewitt would occasionally invite the younger poet round to his house for what Professor Smith calls "tea, Bushmills and gossip".

One of the few things they could agree on, apparently, was the stifling atmosphere in the deeply divided capital city of Northern Ireland. No wonder they both yearned to set off across the water – one to Hull and the other to Coventry.

Hewitt seemed to find the place a breath of fresh air after Belfast. Larkin may have dismissed as alien to him the rebuilding of the city of his birth where, remember, his former home was to be buried under part of the ring road. But the Irish poet seemed entranced by the place as "delightfully open-minded and cosmopolitan".

Professor Smith quotes from a piece that he wrote for the Belfast Telegraph soon after his arrival in which he waxed lyrical about "this remarkable city of surprises and contrasts". Coventry was to him "a triumph of municipal planning and urban renewal". He even compared Britain's first traffic-free precinct to "a piazza in Venice".

I say, steady on old chap, as they rarely say in Belfast. Or, to put it another way, yeah . . . right.

Try as I may, St Mark's Square doesn't come to mind when I step out of Waterstones and glance at the fountain between the upper and lower precincts. As for the Canal Basin, it would have been a bit more work-a-day in Hewitt's time. And anyway it's on the other side of the ring road.

When he wasn't singing the praises of his new home, Hewitt set about creating a gallery and museum to suit local tastes. "His foremost aim [at the Herbert] was to establish a unique assembly of contemporary work – 'British Life and Landscape' – intended to reflect everyday life and thus attract 'the factory worker and his family whose thoughts will seldom if ever be caught up in the complicated tangle of aesthetic theory'," to quote Smith quoting Hewitt, before adding his own interpretation of the poet's motives: "It was also a blueprint for selling modern art to a sceptical council."

There was certainly some scepticism among readers of the Coventry Evening Telegraph when the Herbert acquired a Barbara Hepworth bronze called Walnut and an abstract painting by her husband Ben Nicholson. "Hewitt was slated in the letters page," says the current "curatorial manager", Martin Roberts.

Well over half a century on and both works have stood the test of time. The Walnut is prominently displayed among the sculptures on the first floor and Nicholson's abstract hangs in the nearby Art Since 1900 gallery, close to two unusual works by LS Lowry. Both were set a long way from industrial Lancashire and both were bought to Coventry by Hewitt.

One is of Ebbw Vale in 1960 when it was still home to the largest steelworks in Europe and, to lapse into Larkinese, some loquacious "leftie" called Michael Foot had just become the local MP. "We lent it to Tate Modern for a retrospective a few years ago and it drew lots of attention," Martin confided. The other is of the churchyard at Northleach. In the Cotswolds of all places.

Even more unusual for Lowry, there are no stick figures featured; just the church and the graveyard. Larkin may well have approved of that particular Herbert purchase, bearing in mind his interest in country churches and his early yearning to be helped "down cemetery road".

It's hard to imagine him being quite so impressed by the stunningly colourful Graham Sutherland abstract that dominates the far wall in here. It's one of quite a few Sutherlands harboured at the Herbert. They were woven in France as artist and weavers limbered up for the Big One – Christ in Glory that soars above the alter at the cathedral across the way.

The local weaving tradition is recognised in the History Gallery downstairs, which spans Coventry from mediaeval times to the present day. Local weavers came together in the mid-19th century to put on a display of their collective talents for the Great Exhibition of 1851. Nowhere near as large-scale as the output of Sutherland's French friends, but impressively intricate all the same.

Just round the corner from the History Gallery is a room full of naked ladies on horseback. Well, different artists' impressions of the same lady, and I'm sure I don't have to tell you her name.

The most prominently displayed and, according to Martin, "probably our most viewed picture" is by John Collier. No, not the John Collier that those of us of a certain age will recall as "the fifty shilling tailor". This John Collier (1850-1934) was an artist who painted in Pre-Raphaelite style. In this picture at least, mediaeval Coventry does look more like Venice, or even Florence.

Godiva herself looks young. Too young for my liking. Girlish and virginal, in other words, unlike the more womanly figures in pictures nearby, done by other artists at other times.

At one end of the Godiva Gallery is an entertaining cartoon, played on a loop, about her life and times. At the other end are some evocative old films of Godiva processions past, including at least one from the 1930s when Philip and Sydney Larkin would have been gazing down from their leering point on a Council House balcony.

Philip's memories of Coventry may also have included the hugely impressive picture of Bacchus and Ariadne by Luca Giordano that now takes up the whole of one wall in the Old Masters Gallery upstairs. Before the war it hung first in St Mary's Hall and then in the nearby Gulson Library where Larkin spent so much time.

Yes, the painting was badly damaged in the Blitz but was lovingly restored, as befits a work with such a chequered history.

It was completed in 1677 as a variation on a famous work by Titian, painted 150 years previously and now in the National Gallery in London. But it was originally commissioned to cover a wall in the palazzo of the Rosso family in Florence.

So how on earth did it end up in Coventry?

A local MP, one Edward Ellice, acquired it in 1855. "One story is that it was in part-payment for a gambling debt," Martin revealed. Just over a century later the city finally acquired an art gallery worthy of such a work. For that we owe a debt to the man who gave his name to the building. Not to mention a hundred thousand quid to build it. And that was in 1938. We all know what happened next and indeed what happened to Coventry as a result.

Sir Alfred Herbert was finally able to lay the foundation stone in 1954. Unfortunately, he died three years later, which meant that his wife had to do the formalities when the building finally opened its doors in 1960. She was a different Lady Herbert, incidentally, from the one who gave her name to the formal gardens laid out behind the Hippodrome when Larkin was a lad. Today they still provide a green and peaceful oasis between the Transport Museum on Millennium Square and a ring road full of cars no longer made in Coventry.

In Sir Alfred's day, needless to say, many cars were made here. Bikes too. He had made his money by building up what would become one of the biggest machine-tool companies in the world. Based eventually at Edgwick on the north side of the city, Herbert's were making profits of some six hundred thousand pounds by the 1930s, which amounts to nearly thirty million at today's values.

There were over ten thousand employees and those at the sharp end had been through gruelling apprenticeships that would open any door if they applied for a job elsewhere.

Sir Alfred would make occasional appearances in the tool room, chat amicably with his more venerable employees and cadge a Woodbine from one or another of them. But he'd also check that no lights had been left on.

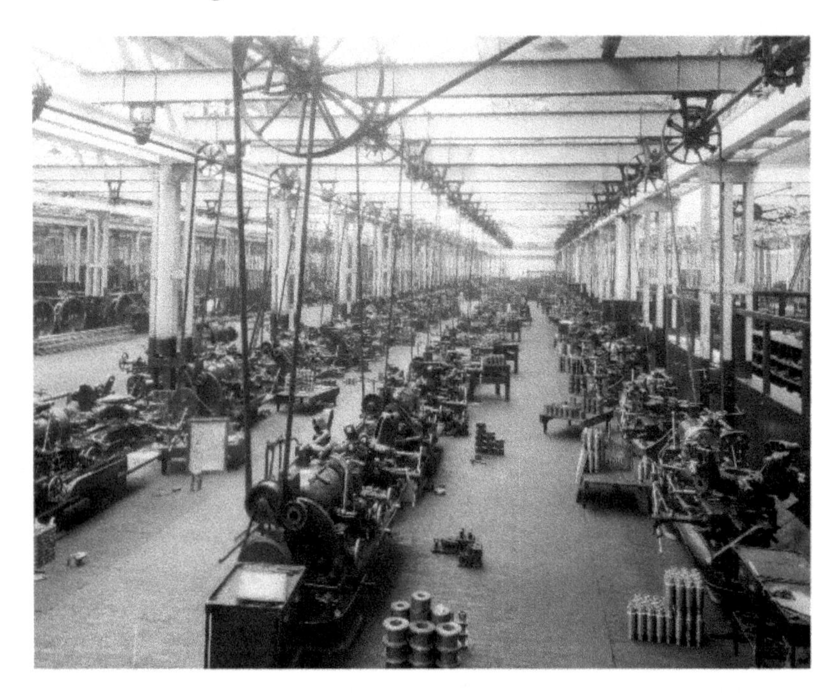

Inside the Alfred Herbert works in 1930
(History Centre)

His philosophy of looking after the pennies also extended to those working in his offices. A friend who was a secretary there once told me that pencils used for shorthand and worn down almost to the last half-inch were expected to be given a life extension by shoving the remaining stub into the end of a cigarette holder.

Such parsimony on an industrial scale would have appealed to Sydney Larkin, I suspect. Sir Alfred was one of those people whom he would have crept around deferentially.

After all, Larkin senior was City Treasurer and the Herbert hundred grand meant that Coventry would – eventually – have a municipal museum and art gallery without the municipality having to shell out too much money. Initially at least.

The building that Sir Alfred bequeathed was of its time, modernist with Festival-of-Britain aspects about it. Twenty first century additions have improved it no end. Apart from the stylish glass extension, there are new spaces for visiting exhibitions and access has been provided to the surviving mediaeval undercroft.

There's a spacious café, what's more. Anybody sitting at one of the tables in the adjoining courtyard in fine weather might notice a plaque on a wall near the side entrance. It's dedicated to "John Hewitt, Irish poet [and] art director at this gallery 1957-72". Well merited. His legacy lives on inside. The 'modern art' that he purchased has stood the test of time.

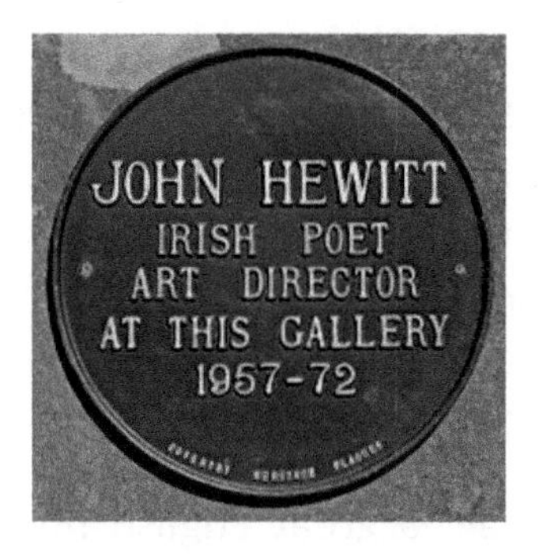

Another plaque to another poet who was far more enthusiastic than Larkin about post-war Coventry

Had he still been alive, I doubt that Philip Larkin, English poet, born in Coventry in 1922, would have been greatly impressed by the Herbert winning The Guardian's 2010 award for being family-friendly and making children welcome. After all, he took his mother's advice and had no kids himself.

Yet I find the place a godsend if I'm looking after one or more of my grandkids on a wet day. And even if I'm on my own or with my wife, I still like dropping in. After all, it's in my favourite part of the city centre with the cathedral just across the square, St Mary's Hall and Castle Yard nearby and Draper's Bar across the road.

And there's a thriving university next door, what's more. The "youthful vibrancy" brought here by so many students from all over the world is oft-quoted as a reason for Coventry being honoured as the City of Culture, 2021.

I'm "cool" about that. Oh yeah, I can get "down with the kids". Still, as I may have mentioned earlier, the city's literary heritage should not be overlooked. Talking of which . . .

In the 19th century section of the Herbert's History Gallery is a small collection of items connected to George Eliot, including a desk and an intricately carved card table. There's also a portrait of the novelist by Dorade. "We may be doing something more expansive for the bi-centenary of her birth next year (2019)," mused Martin, the Hewitt *de nos jours*.

She was, after all, a great English novelist of the 19th century with strong Coventry influences, as discussed in an earlier chapter. What's more, as this book was going to press, the Herbert was staging a major exhibition of the major work of a major 20th century poet also called Eliot. TS, no less. The Waste Land explores Eliot's famous poem in the context of Coventry's history as a city fragmented by war and rebuilt upon its ruins.

It remains to be seen whether the forthcoming City of Culture will do much to mark the centenary of the birth of another major 20th century poet who just happened to spend his first 18 years here.

No, we shouldn't celebrate his views – on life, up skirts or down cleavage. But at a time when Kipling's most popular poem, If, can be defaced by students in Manchester because he was an "imperialist" and a "racist", it is perhaps time to point out once again that literary talent is something separate from the political outlook of men or women of their time. It seems unlikely that Shakespeare holding forth over a tankard of sack in the Globe Inn would tick all the boxes of 21st century political correctness.

Yet it's fair to say that the town where he spent his early life and final years has made the most of his name. And before you ask, no I'm not comparing Larkin with the Bard. Nor am I decrying the fact that Larkin is now remembered on platform one of Coventry Station, a paving slab in Priory Place, a pub sign on the corner of the Burges and, indeed, on the road sign of a cul-de-sac in the suburb of Walsgrave.

But a few readings in Coventry libraries and other public spheres wouldn't go amiss in 2021. And why shouldn't some of his work be included in the planned poetic celebration of the ring road under which his former family home is buried?

I'd also like to see some of his devastating last lines bedecking some appropriate parts of the city, including "What will survive of us is love" and, yes, "Nothing, like something, happens anywhere". Just as long as it's preceded by "'I suppose it's not the place's fault,' I said."

It most definitely was not.

BIBLIOGRAPHY

Amis, Martin: Philip Larkin Poems (Faber and Faber, 2011)

Booth, James: Philip Larkin, Life Art and Love (Bloomsbury, 2014)

Bradford, Richard: First Boredom, Then Fear. The Life of Philip Larkin (Peter Owen, 2005)

Bradford, Richard: The Importance of Elsewhere, Philip Larkin's Photography (Frances Lincoln, 2015)

Hartley, Jean: Philip Larkin, the Marvell Press and Me (The Sumach Press, 1993)

King, Francis: EM Forster and his World (Thames and Hudson, 1978)

Kynaston, David: Modernity Britain 1957-62 (Bloomsbury, 2015)

Larkin, Philip: Early Poems and Juvenalia (Faber and Faber, 2005)

Larkin, Philip: Jill (Faber and Faber, 1964; first published 1946)

Larkin, Philip: The Less Deceived (Marvell Press, 1955)

Larkin, Philip: The Whitsun Weddings (Marvell Press, 1964, republished by Faber and Faber, 2001)

Moss, Sarah: The Tidal Zone (Granta, 2016)

Priestley JB: English Journey (Mandarin, 1994; first published 1934)

Pullen, Philip: No Villainous Mother – The Life of Eva Larkin from Writers and their mothers (Palgrave Macmillan, 2018)

Smith, Adrian: The City of Coventry: A Twentieth Century Icon (IB Taurus, 2005)

Walters, Peter: The Story of Coventry (The History Press, 2013)

Lightning Source UK Ltd.
Milton Keynes UK
UKHW021151131118
332256UK00005B/587/P